The Way Beyond

Cover design by *Jane A. Evans*

Cover photo by Joy Mills
Other photos by Benita Mikulas

The Way Beyond

An Overview of Spiritual Practices

William L. Mikulas

*This publication made possible with
the assistance of the Kern Foundation*

The Theosophical Publishing House
Wheaton, Ill. U.S.A.
Madras, India/London, England

The Theosophical Publishing House
306 West Geneva Road
Wheaton, IL 60187

A publication of the Theosophical Publishing House, a department of the Theosophical Society in America.

Library of Congress Cataloging in Publication Data

Mikulas, William L.
    The way beyond.
    (A Quest book)
    "A Quest original"—T.p. verso.
    Bibliography: p.
    1. Spiritual life. I. Title.
BL624.M49 1987   158'.1   87-40131
ISBN 0-8356-0625-2 (pbk.)

Printed in the United States of America

For Benita

Contents

1

Overview

This book is a guide to help you plan the most significant journey you can take. The purpose is to provide you with a practical overview and handbook of fundamental transpersonal and spiritual practices that have been developed throughout the world. When you have such a broad overview, you can more effectively choose those practices and teachings which are best suited for your current position and goals. There is a multitude of good books that provide detailed discussions of various transpersonal theories and practices. This book is more general and provides an integration of the basic practices used in these various approaches.

So, who is going on this journey? Some travelers primarily think about the journey psychologically. They are interested in things such as maximizing their potential, self-actualization, peak experiences and peak performance, and psychological insights. Other travelers wish to move beyond ("trans") the limitations of their conditioned personal beings. Their transpersonal journey or consciousness exploration is aimed at getting beyond the restrictions and suffering of an ego-based reality. Some existentialists suggest there is a basic force or will for such self-transcendence. Other travelers perceive themselves on a spiritual journey, perhaps wishing some type of experience, communion, or merging with that which is greater than themselves and which "includes" them.

We could describe many other perspectives; it seems that most people are on some type of quest that leads them to science, psychology, philosophy, religion, or the occult in the hopes of satisfying some basic yearnings. In the next four chapters, I describe four different ways of thinking about the universal journey.

Although there are many different ways to think about the journey and where it leads, there is agreement among the great traditions about the most effective *practices* for traveling on the journey. This book is a survey of these practices and related issues. This is a book about what to *do*, not what to believe. In fact, relative to the journey it is often best to "believe" as little as possible. Just follow the practices, go on the journey, and see for yourself.

The benefits of the practices are many and include the following: clearing of perception, increased mental flexibility and creativity, transcendence of assumptions and limitations, new insights about self and world, and greater happiness and peace of mind. Life becomes simpler, lighter, and more direct. One becomes more effective at helping other people achieve the same.

In this book I describe the fundamental essence of the practices and how they relate to each other. When this is understood you can more intelligently pursue other sources (books, teachers, training programs, etc.) for more detail and elaboration of the practices.

Transpersonal/spiritual practices are potentially

very powerful. This should not be underestimated. They can literally transform your being. Therefore, I must include the following warning: if any such practices cause unpleasant psychological disturbances, then stop the practices and consult a counselor or guide who is experienced in that area. Occasionally, a person's ego may be overwhelmed by the thoughts and images that arise during meditation. Or you may be upset by the boredom and frustration that may occur during part of the journey. And in yoga, some practices may produce a variety of sensations that could be upsetting to someone who does not understand them.

Finally, it would be useful here to make two distinctions: between "form" and "essence," and between "religious" and "spiritual." In this book essence refers to the fundamental nature of a practice or act, while form refers to the particular manifestation or example of the essence. Thus, when I discuss the essence of concentration, I am referring to a fundamental property of the mind (how focused or one-pointed it is) independent of the form the concentration takes (what the mind is focused on and related experiences). Thus, the *practice* of developing the *essence* of concentration is universal, even though the *form* of the practice may vary considerably. Thus, the form might involve sitting meditation or listening exercises, while the essence of what is being developed is the same. This book deals with the essence of basic personal and transpersonal practices, with various forms used as examples.

Confusing form with essence is a common trap for people on the journey. For example, an American who wishes to pursue a Hindu or Buddhist path may get lost in the form of the practice (con-

4

cepts, culture, dress, vocabulary, etc.) and miss the essence of the practice which is universally independent of form. Now it may be practical and/or desirable to choose a particular form, but the form is only useful to the extent it facilitates developing or manifesting the essence.

People have described transpersonal experiences and insights within the forms of science, philosophy, religion, poetry, paintings, music, and teaching stories. But there is a universal essence to what is being described, some of which is called the Perennial Philosophy (see appendices), regardless of the various forms.

Similarly with the distinction between spiritual and religious: I use the term "spiritual" to refer to those practices, insights, states of being, and frames of reference related to that which is superordinate to, prior to, and inclusive of the individual. The essence of the spiritual is often found within the form of religion. By "religious," I refer to those beliefs, rituals, and social customs which are the result of spiritual, political, and cultural forces. Thus, this is a spiritual book, not a religious book. It deals with spiritual practices, not religious beliefs. However, many of the spiritual practices will be described in forms drawn from the world religions. From a spiritual point of view the beliefs and devotional practices of a particular religion are helpful to the extent that they lead in a transpersonal direction, and harmful to the extent that they bind people to the form or politics. Even those religions which argue that there is nothing to do and/or that faith is sufficient advocate certain ways of being which are facilitated by the spiritual practices.

The essence of the spiritual and transpersonal

practices is very simple and universal. But the depth and breadth hidden in this simplicity is continually uncovered as one continues the journey.

I
Perspectives

2

The Self

Since the journey leads beyond the self and is based on getting free from a self-defined reality, it is important to understand what the self is and how it came to be.

A newborn baby must learn to perceive the world. Although entering the world with the ability to sense many things, such as basic sounds and smells, the child must learn how to perceive. For example, in the case of vision, the child must learn how to move and focus the eyes, pick out particular forms, see shapes within shapes, and store some of this information in memory for future comparison.

The culture influences this learning by affecting what the child is exposed to and what the child is rewarded for perceiving. The culture also teaches the child a language with which to label and categorize perceptions. Eventually, the child's perception and thinking are strongly influenced by language.

The child's consciousness at first is quite undifferentiated. Sensations rise and fall, but there is little of the discriminating, categorizing, judging, and accepting and rejecting that is common to the adult mind. Similarly, at first there is little sense of a personal self, a division of experiences into me and not-me. The child is said to be in a pre-

personal stage, a stage of development before a sense of a personal, individualized self.

Then the child gradually develops a sense of self. At first this is influenced by the discovery of the body as something that can be controlled to some degree and as different from things outside the body. So the early sense of self is to some extent identified with the body.

Associated with the sense of self is a sense of will, the action or influence of the self. As the self develops and changes, so does the will. American mothers often talk about the "terrible twos," referring to the fact that children around two years of age often practice exerting their developing self and will. This may take the form of being willful, controlling, or opinionated.

As a sense of self or "me" develops, so does a sense of "mine." Not only does the child have a sense of an individualized self, but this self also possesses things in the world.

As this is happening, the child moves from the prepersonal stage to the *personal stage,* the stage of development centering around the self and will. This is the "fall from Eden," the gradual "getting lost" in an ego-based reality.

Now a person's sense of self continually changes. As we get older and watch our body change, we identify less with the body. Rather, the body is perceived as being part of the self, or as something the self inhabits or controls.

Our sense of self may become more identified with the mind and/or social roles. A child asked to answer the question "Who am I?" may answer in terms of body and name, while an older person may answer in terms of social roles, such as vocation and family position. By now the person is

probably strongly identified with some sense of self which is the thinker of thoughts, perceiver of perceptions, doer of actions, and consistent subject of many memories.

Thus, many people identify with the activity of their minds: "I am the thinker of these thoughts." Others develop a sense of inner self in which the self is more of an observer: "I am the observer of the mind having thoughts. I am not the thinker of the thoughts, I am the observer of the thinker."

Regardless of these distinctions, most adults have a sense of a separate self that exists in some relation to their bodies. Most people I have polled feel that "they" are inside their heads. Some feel they are inside their hearts, diffused through the whole body, or just above or behind the head.

Two important psychological phenomena commonly occur during the personal stage of development. One is that the person acquires a variety of thoughts, feelings, and attitudes toward the self, many of which are often negative in tone. Secondly, the person's self may fractionate into several different selves and/or aspects of the self.

During development, our sense of self is continually being conditioned by parents, peers, television, and so forth. We come to believe we are smart or stupid, attractive or plain, worthy or unworthy, and so on. Thus, a person develops a self-concept and self-esteem. Now, surprisingly, our self-concept often is not very accurate. For example, a person who is generally perceived by others as clever and charming may perceive himself as being slow and dull. Many of the humanistic therapies focus on our unrealistic and/or overly negative associations to our self.

Many people are more tolerant and accepting of friends than of themselves. Thus, a recurrent theme in this book will be to "make friends with yourself." This involves clearly seeing your strengths and weaknesses and unconditionally accepting them all, as you hopefully would with a good friend, while also recognizing ways to improve and trying to do so.

When a person dislikes some aspect of the perceived self, the self may be broken into parts and some parts pushed out of consciousness. Thus, the self becomes fragmented.

Similarly, a person may develop different selves for different situations, such as a parent self, an employee self, and a party self. Problems arise when we have trouble integrating these different selves into one self. For example, a person may have trouble combining the tough, hard-headed business person with the warm, compassionate lover and parent, although these are not necessarily incompatible. Some Western therapies, such as Gestalt therapy and Psychosynthesis, and some tantric and Tibetan Buddhist practices are designed to synthesize and integrate the various aspects of the different selves.

What I have described can be seen in the following common example: Parents want their child to be in some way different from the way he or she is. A part of the child's mind assumes the parents' position and then negatively evaluates other aspects of self. The child's self is then split, and suffering results.

An important point to keep in mind is that, as a general rule, before we can adequately move into the next stage of development, we must resolve many of the issues of the personal stage. We need to uncover and synthesize different aspects of the self, and to make friends with ourselves.

The next stage of development after the personal stage is the *transpersonal stage*. Here the person gets beyond the limitations and problems which result from identifying with a particular, restricted, individualized sense of self. It is not that the self ceases to exist or loses its functions; rather one transcends the identification with the self. This transcendence opens the person to greater clarity, freedom, and peace of mind. The fundamental essence of the self sits at the border between the personal and transpersonal. When one sees through the self, one sees into the transpersonal.

Ramana Maharshi, a respected Indian yogi, suggested the inquiry "Who am I?" as a major practice for moving from the personal to the transpersonal. The practice involves continually tuning the consciousness toward the subjective experience of the self. Who is reading these words? What is your direct, first-hand experience of this self who is reading? Who is the observer of the self? This is a powerful practice that leads to ever subtler levels of the apparent self.

Similarly, Buddhist *vipassana* meditation practices lead to a direct experience and insight into the nature of the self. When the mind is sufficiently calm and aware, it is turned on the experience of self. What is found is that there is no constant, unchanging entity of self; rather there is a dynamic set of processes of grasping and contraction. Seeing through this is liberating.

But all of this is getting too far ahead. This book surveys those practices which help to resolve issues at the personal stage and lead to the transpersonal. You can see the exact nature of the self and the transpersonal for "yourself" later in the journey.

3

Levels of Being

There are four levels of being human: the biological, the behavioral, the personal, and the transpersonal. These four levels are totally interrelated and exist in practically everyone, whether we are aware of them or not.

The biological level, the level of the body including the brain, is the exquisite product of dynamic forces that can be viewed evolutionarily and/or teleologically. Its form and nature are the result of the interplay of genetic, environmental, and learning factors. It strongly influences the other three levels and depends on them for most effective functioning.

The biological level is the species level, what it means to be *homo sapiens*. This includes what we as a species are capable of sensing; our limitations are in what we are capable of seeing, hearing, smelling, tasting, and feeling. For example, the visual spectrum is a very small part of the electromagnetic spectrum. Yet we readily develop a sense of "reality" based on what is perceived through these small windows.

The major characteristic of the human species is that it was biologically selected for its capability to learn, with predispositions for certain types of learning, such as for language. Through learning, humans can adapt to various situations without requiring biological changes in the species. Through learning, humans can communicate, store, and transmit knowledge and, thereby, develop cultures.

The biological level is the level of many individual differences including physical characteristics, reactivity of the nervous system, chemical balances in the brain, and variability of blood sugar level. These and a host of other biological factors can influence emotions, thinking ability, sense of well-being, and ability to maximize processes of the other three levels.

Good breathing, exercise, and nutrition are stressed by many spiritual disciplines. This includes learning deep breathing and the influence of breathing on biological, psychological, and spiritual states. This has been particularly well developed in the yoga of India and the Taoism of China. Exercise strengthens the cardiovascular system and improves flexibility and muscle tone. Appropriate exercise also improves mood, promoting peacefulness of mind. Good nutrition involves establishing a healthy diet and learning how different foods influence energy, mood, and psycho-spiritual state. There are great individual differences here. *Ayurvedic* nutrition in yoga has much to contribute.

The second level of being human is the behavioral level, which deals with the output of the biological level. What do the body and brain do? Behaviors include moving, talking, emoting, and thinking. Thus the behavioral level includes how we act, feel, and think. Specific behaviors are a function of biological factors interacting with learning and motivation. Behavior modification is an effective current Western therapy for dealing with behaviors, and changes at the behavioral level often produce changes at the biological level.

The third level, the personal, is the level of subjective consciousness, which includes the subjective experience of the first two levels. Somehow related to the behaving body/mind is a sense of conscious awareness. It is the level of mind and perception, as opposed to brain and sensation. I am aware of the thinking and imaging of my mind, however it may be related to the physical brain. I am aware of my perceptions of seeing, however they may be related to visual sensations affecting the eye and brain. The limitations of the biological level and the dynamics of the behavioral level greatly influence what gets into consciousness at the personal level.

Here also is the seat of the personal self discussed in the last chapter. For not only is there consciousness, but the consciousness is often from the vantage point of an individualized self and related will. And this self-based consciousness can also be aware of itself to some extent. I can examine my sense of self. So we say there is self-consciousness.

Being the seat of the self, the personal level is also the domain of self-concept, self-esteem, self-determination, self-control, self-efficacy, and so forth.

Although such self-based experiences can sometimes be changed by interventions aimed at the personal level, they are often most effectively changed via changes at the biological and behavioral level. Thus, a person with a poor self-concept may not be best helped by confronting the self-concept. Rather, it may be better to help the person learn new social and vocational skills, learn better control of thoughts, and overcome specific behavioral problems. This will lead to more effective and happy living which will usually improve the self-concept. Thus all the great spiritual traditions recognize the importance of ordering one's life on moral and practical guidelines and cleaning up one's life at the biological and behavioral levels to facilitate changes at the personal and transpersonal levels.

Conversely, changes at the personal level, such as improving attitudes toward the self or synthesizing disparate aspects of the self, often produce changes at the behavioral and biological levels. Resolving personal level issues increases awareness of body and behavior, reduces stress, and breaks down some of the apparent barriers between levels. And changes at the personal level are often necessary or useful before one can most effectively work at the transpersonal level.

At the boundary of the personal level and the transpersonal level is the very essence of the self. Existentialists often confront the self and related will around issues concerning individual existence. Topics of importance to many existentialists include personal autonomy, authenticity, self-actualization, mortality, aloneness, meaning, responsibility, and freedom. Imbedded here are many potential sources of anxiety, such as that related to boundaries of being, feelings of isolation, threat of death, sense of fundamental impotence, and perceived absurdity. These existential anxieties are often not resolvable at the personal level, but are transcended in the transpersonal level.

The fourth level, the transpersonal, is beyond and "prior to" the personal level. It is the field of forces in which the apparent self emerges and changes. It is consciousness per se, rather than the contents of consciousness of the personal level. It is pure existence prior to the form of existence. It is a state-of-being of fundamental peace and equanimity, as opposed to the pleasure and pain of the other levels. It is the ground in which one's vantage point is no longer identified with the individualized self of the personal level.

Although everyone exists at the transpersonal level, most people most of the time are constricted in their awareness to the personal level. It is usually only in special circumstances, such as the birth of a child or a religious experience, that one consciously touches the transpersonal. But this level is always there. Thus, it is not something to be acquired or achieved, only realized. It is not something that the self can experience or possess since it is beyond the self. Developmentally, most people move from the prepersonal stage to the personal stage, and they basically get stuck there, unaware of the transpersonal level of their being. Continued development into the transpersonal stage involves the freeing realization of the transpersonal level, which was always present.

It is difficult to describe the transpersonal in terms of traditional conceptual knowledge, for the transpersonal level is based on insights and knowledge that is of a type different from conceptual knowledge. Transpersonal knowledge is usually validated in a way that seems immediately obvious, like the "ah-ha" experience.

This book provides various conceptualizations of the transpersonal. Yet the transpersonal is not adequately approached or understood conceptually, so the concepts are useful only to the extent that they lead beyond themselves to other types of knowing. There is no particular idea, concept, theory, or belief that I am arguing for. You as a reader will agree or disagree with different statements, choosing what is useful to you. Find and develop those ideas and related practices which speak to you. But be careful that clinging to particular ideas or beliefs doesn't impair your progress into broader domains of knowing and being.

4

The Game of Life

Consider popular games like Monopoly, back-
gammon, and bridge. How well one does in these
games is a combination of skill and luck. For
many of us the amount of fun we have playing
such games depends on whether we win or not. If
we are winning, we enjoy the game much more
than if we are losing. And some people gloat
when they win and complain when they lose.

There is another less common type of game
player. For this player, whom I call a meta-player,
the fun is in the playing of the game, not in winning or losing. The meta-player tries to win, since
that is the objective of the game, but the fun is in
playing the game, win or lose. Thus the meta-
player always has a good time, while the happiness of the average player cycles up and down.

Next, consider the game of life, the adventure-
drama of daily living. Everyone has ideas about
what constitutes winning here. Winning might be
measured in terms of money, prestige, friends,
health, pleasure, or spiritual progress. Most people sometimes win in the game of life and sometimes lose. Like most games, the game of life has
components of both skill and luck. Some things
you can control and master; some things you
can't.

For everyone who plays the game of life it is

important to learn to play the game well, to play skillfully, with clarity, precision, and compassion. We need to acquire the knowledge and skills to maximize winning and to increase the role of skill over luck. Unfortunately, for the average player happiness depends on the amount of winning, but for the meta-player happiness is based on simply playing the game. The meta-player considers the game very important and does his best to win. But the meta-player enjoys and appreciates just the opportunity to play.

The game of life is filled with pleasure and pain, and a common objective of the game is to maximize pleasure and minimize pain. All this is fine at the level of the game. But the common trap is to allow our happiness to be dependent on the amount of pleasure in the game. Happiness is better based on how you play the game, rather than the outcome of the game. This is the "secret" of the meta-player. As one learns this, one gradually gets free from the game, which is the key to the transpersonal. So there is pleasure and pain at the level of the game, and happiness at the level of how you play the game. Beyond this, one finds a peace of mind which is totally independent of the game.

Similarly, the game of life is filled with potential sources of stress that can impair the body and mind. The average player experiences considerable stress in the game, while the meta-player experiences much less stress and can often transform potential sources of stress into sources of energy.

In the first chapter, I made a distinction between "religious" and "spiritual." In terms of the analogy of this chapter, we can say that religion is

at the level of the game, while spirituality is involved with getting free from the game.

In many games it is possible occasionally to call a time-out and step out of the game for a while. This gives you a chance to catch your breath, see the game more objectively, and re-evaluate your game strategy. Unfortunately, few players ever take time-out from the game of life; they just keep playing. They may change aspects of the game, such as the setting, but they are always in the game. In this book you will learn how meditation is a way to call time-out in the game of life. And the chapter on retreats discusses additional ways.

Another type of game on the market today is the role-playing and/or fantasy game, such as "Dungeons and Dragons." In these games the player may assume a role, such as that of wizard, pirate, mafia boss, or extra-terrestial. Thus, a player may be a pirate while in the game, but step out of this role during time-outs and when the game is over. Occasionally problems arise when a player has trouble totally getting out of the role he assumed for the game.

The game of life is a role-playing game in which you have been taught a specific role by parents, friends, teachers, and your culture. As in all role-playing games, it is important to really get into this role and have fun playing it as best you can. The problem with the game of life is that people get so caught up in their roles that they begin to believe and defend them. They get lost in the melodrama and start believing that the game is basic reality. The meta-player sees through this, recognizes the restricted "reality" of the game, and does not identify the "self" with the role.

24

When a person sees through or wakes up from the role-playing game of life, he realizes that whoever he is it isn't the role. He becomes less vulnerable, for he can't be hurt in many of the ways the character in the game can be hurt. He realizes that a person is not his behavior. Our essence is different from our actions. We can learn the importance of loving ourselves and others unconditionally, regardless of how we or others behave in the game. We may like and dislike some of our own and others' behaviors and may try to change some of them. That is fine at the level of the game, but beyond this is the unconditional acceptance and love of all players, many of whom are lost in the game.

For practical reasons, most people must continue to play their roles in the game, although they can significantly alter the roles. The trick is to be able to continually play the game but not be lost in it. This is the great spiritual teaching that one should be "in the world but not of it," emphasized by the Christ, the Buddha, the Sufis, and others.

5

Dreaming

When you are asleep and dreaming, the dream can seem very real; you are living in a different reality, a different state of consciousness. The rules of reality in the dream are different from the rules of the normal non-sleep consensus reality. In the dream, people may pop in and out of existence or change into other people or other beings. In the dream, you may be able to do miraculous things or be many different people. The sense of self can be very different from the sense of self in the normal non-sleep conscious state.

Sometimes you might "wake up" in the dream; that is, you might still be dreaming but be aware that you are dreaming and that the dream is not "real." This is called "lucid" dreaming. People can learn how to wake up more often in dreams and thus profit more from the dream state. They can then alter the dreams in various ways. Similarly, a hypnogogic state of consciousness may occur as a person starts to fall asleep; this is the drowsy place between awake and asleep. Here a person may have an awake type of conscious awareness of dream-like mental activity beginning to occur.

So people can be awake in varying degrees during sleeping dreams. But for most people most of the time, when they are dreaming they are lost in

the apparent reality of the dream. When they wake up, they see the dream for what it is: the mental activity of a particular state of consciousness, a subset of a broader reality.

Now consider the next step, waking up from the normal awake consciousness. What would it be like to wake up from this consensus reality, wake up from this ego-based level of consciousness? In fact, throughout recorded history everywhere in the world there have been people so awakening. To these awakened beings, normal conscious reality is like a dream. It seems very real to most people, but once you awaken it is seen for what it is: the mental activity of a particular state of consciousness, a subset of a broader reality.

Some people who are lost in the waking-dream of normal consciousness may occasionally be aware they are dreaming. Some dreamers may even learn ways to wake up *in* the dream. But for the person who has awakened from the dream, it is clear that all one has to do is wake up. Much of what one does in the dream itself is related only to the melodrama of the dream, not to waking up from the dream.

This leads to a fundamental spiritual truth: there is nothing you must do *in order to* awaken, just *wake up*. Activities within the dream are still within the dream; it is a matter of waking from the dream. The self can improve itself and collect experiences and ideas; but this does not necessarily ever lead beyond the self. Zen is founded on this spiritual truth. Zen teachers and practices are continually confounding the student's attempt to achieve something within the dream. Rather, Zen continually exposes the student to the awakened perspective, which is everyone's fundamental ground.

Now simply being told to wake up is not very helpful. What is the dreamer to do? Fortunately, the answer is clear. The dreamer follows those practices which improve life within the dream and set the stage for awakening. This book summarizes such practices.

Thus, the seemingly paradoxical truth is that the dreamer carries out practices within the dream that facilitate awakening from the dream, which in turn leads to the realization that nothing had to occur in the dream in order for one to be awakened.

The awakened state has been described in many terms including enlightenment, *satori*, cosmic consciousness, Christ consciousness, consciousness-without-an-object, at-one-ment, illumination, and return to the source. Although these terms are not equivalent, the fundamental perspective of awakened beings is universal. It is a conscious perspective which is prior to and inclusive of the normal state of consciousness. All the descriptive analogies for moving into this transpersonal domain are inaccurate in many ways. But the analogy of waking from a dream is quite useful and popular. Other common analogies include levels of consciousness, rebirth, escape from prison or bonds, and mythical quests.

Few people suddenly wake up. For most it is a case of gradually awakening, with slow, uneven "progress." Sometimes there is a good jump "forward," sometimes a melodramatic fall "backward." Sometimes there is continual "progress," sometimes frustrating stuckness. Eventually the person may have the feeling of waking up, falling asleep, waking up, etc., with the waking up times gradually becoming more frequent, longer, broader, and subtler.

The key here is not to get caught up in the drama of the "progress" of awakening as perceived by the dreamer. This only reinforces the illusionary search within the dream. Rather, one continues the practices within the dream, learns not to equate objectives of the dream with probability of awakening, and continually reorients toward that which is superordinate to the dream.

II
Basic Practices

6

Meditation

The word "meditation" is used to refer to many different things. For some it means to think about or ponder over something ("I'll meditate on that"). For others it means to fantasize or daydream. For still others meditation is necessarily a religious or occult practice. None of these interpretations is what is meant here.

In this book meditation is a "time-out" from "the game of life." It is a time to set the body down and relax the mind. It is an opportunity to work with the processes of the mind and disentangle oneself from the ordinary melodrama.

The fundamental meditation practices of all the world's great meditation traditions can be reduced to two basic components: processes of the mind and objects of attention. All the great traditions emphasize the development of one or both of two fundamental processes of the mind: concentration and mindfulness. These will be discussed in the next two chapters.

The second basic component of meditation, the object of attention, is what the meditator focuses consciousness on, with eyes open or closed. It might be something you look at, such as a photograph or mandala. It might be sounds, such as a prayer, chant, or mantra. Or it might be an image called up in the mind. The object is chosen because of particular properties of the object itself and/or associations it has for the meditator.

In the spiritual exercises of St. Ignatius, the objects of attention are scenes from Christ's life, used as a way of opening to Christ. A yogi might focus on the mantra *aum*, a primordial sound leading one back toward the source. A Tibetan Buddhist might focus on the image of a "deity" which represents a particular aspect or force of the mind. A Theravadin Buddhist might meditate on the death and decay of the body as a means to get free from vain attachment to the body. And Western therapies are filled with imagery techniques in which clients focus on specific imagined scenes. Therapeutic change is attributed to processes such as covert conditioning, modeling, reprogramming the unconscious, and altering expectations.

The multitude of objects of meditation is not within the domain of this book, with a few exceptions to come later. Rather, the emphasis is on the basic form, attitude, and mental processes of meditation. When these are mastered to some extent, the meditator can more profitably choose and utilize various objects of meditation which are more specialized to particular paths and/or individual needs.

Physical Form

The Buddha suggested four basic forms for meditation—sitting, lying, standing, and walking. As sitting is the best form for most people, this is the form I will describe. You can later adapt what is said to other forms. Lying down is a good form for some people, but most are more likely to fall asleep. In the mindfulness chapter I describe a walking meditation.

For sitting meditation, you want to set your body down so that the spine is basically vertical, the body is relaxed and balanced, and you are not leaning in any direction. There are many ways to sit, including on a chair with feet flat on the floor and not leaning against the chair. The most popular position is sitting cross-legged on the floor on a cushion to help provide a firm, stable base. (The lotus position with legs crossed and feet on thighs is good if you can easily do it. The half lotus is too unbalanced.) The key is to have a firm, balanced base so that you can sit for a while without strain or expending much energy. Shift around and settle into a balanced position.

Set your hands in your lap, palms up, with the non-dominant hand on top. If you are right-handed, your right hand is dominant. One way to position the hands is with corresponding fingers on top of each other and thumb tips gently touching. Shoulders should be aligned above the hips, head forward and allowed to hang down, and eyes closed. Take a couple of deep breaths, and then let your breathing go naturally, breathing through the nose as much as possible.

Breath as Object

Now what do you do while sitting like this? Simply observe your breath. Worldwide, the breath is the most used object of meditation. There are many reasons for this. The breath is always there, so it is readily available and a constant reminder when your practice becomes more continuous. There are many lessons to be learned from the breathing, such as how to get out of the way and let things naturally happen. For many people, such as yogis, the breath is seen as a manifestation of the fundamental life energy.

There are many ways to follow the breath. One way is to focus on the breath at the tip of the nose. Notice the air movement through your nose and how it swirls around the tip of your nose when you breath out. Notice how the air coming in is cooler than the air going out. Notice how sometimes you breathe primarily through one nostril.

A second way to follow the breath is to watch the rising and falling of the diaphragm, the partition of muscles and sinews between your chest cavity and stomach cavity. Whereas shallow or frightened breathing mostly involves the chest muscles, healthy relaxed breathing is based on the diaphragm. When the diaphragm rises, it forces air out of the lungs. When the diaphragm falls, air comes into the lungs and the stomach is pushed out. Thus, a third way to follow the breath is by watching the rising and falling of the abdomen itself.

In the next few days practice sitting a number of times as described above, and try watching your breath in the three different ways. Find the one that works best for you, and make that your form of meditation. You can always change later, but it is good not to change around too much, particularly at first. In the Theravadin Buddhist tradition it is suggested that following the breath at the tip of the nose or at the diaphragm is best for quieting the mind (Chapter 7), while watching the abdomen rise and fall is best for mindfulness (Chapter 8).

Setting

Where and when you meditate is important. Have a special place, perhaps with a special cushion or robe. Over time these props may help get you in the right "mood" for meditation. Free yourself from interruptions by taking the phone off the hook, putting out a "do not disturb" sign, etc.

Find your best time of day to meditate, a time when you are relaxed, not tired, and not too hungry or too full. Experiment to find the time that best suits your lifestyle and body cycles. Ideally, it is best if it is about the same time each day. Near the beginning and end of each day are two good times. In the morning after one has risen, used the toilet, and perhaps exercised is a good time as it clears the mind and predisposes one in a positive direction. At the end of the day, before one gets too tired, is another good time as it quiets the mind and allows for the day's activities to be more processed and resolved.

At first it is good if you meditate ten to fifteen minutes a day four or more days a week, then gradually build up to fifteen to thirty minutes a day at least six days a week. If you can meditate more than once a day, that is great.

In fact, just a minute of being quiet and aware is very powerful. But most people, at least for a while, need to sit longer for such minutes occasionally to occur. Also, there will be times when your mood and circumstances encourage you to sit longer than usual, and there may be times you crave meditation simply to relax and re-center yourself.

The Practice

The practice is very simple, although most meditators make it very difficult. All you do is sit down, relax, and watch your breath whenever you can. Now much of the time your mind will be running all over, perceiving, thinking, planning, and remembering. Only some of the time will you actually watch your breath. This is common and to be expected.

However, you do not want to actively encourage this mental activity or choose to let yourself get lost in it. Rather, you want just to notice any mental activity and return to your breath whenever you can.

Similarly, many sounds, body feelings, and other sensations will arise and attract your attention. Whenever this happens, simply notice the sensation and return to your breath. If you have to move, such as readjusting your legs or scratching your nose, simply move, notice all related sensations, and return to your breath.

Various insights and new ideas may arise during meditation, such as solutions to problems or new perspectives on yourself or others. Whenever these arise, simply notice them and return to the breath.

For a few people, some of the things that arise during meditation can be disturbing. If this happens to you, stop meditating until you consult a qualified meditation teacher and/or psychological counselor.

So the practice is very simple. You just sit and watch your breath; no matter what arises in your consciousness, you simply note it and return to your breath. Often what arises will pull you into itself, so that it is a while before you return to your breath. No problem; this is common and natural. Just return to your breath when you can. Don't worry about how often any of this happens; just return to your breath whenever you can.

When you return to the breath, it is a matter of

gently and firmly bringing your attention back to the direct experience of breathing at the chosen point of focus, such as the tip of the nose. It is not thinking about breathing or thinking about where your attention was. It simply is returning to the experience of breathing. Don't try to hold your attention on your breathing; that won't work. Just bring your attention back when you can.

An effective way to help focus your attention on your breathing is through the simple labeling of "in-out" or "rising-falling." When following the breath at the tip of the nose, silently say "in" to yourself when breathing in and "out" when breathing out. If you are watching the rising and falling of your diaphragm or abdomen, use the words "rising" and "falling." If you wish to use a mantra, you can use the yogic liberation mantra *"So Ham"* ("I am That") or the Buddhist mantra *"Budd-ho."* In the first, you would say *So* (pronounced SOH) on the outbreath and *HAM* (pronounced HUM) on the inbreath. In the latter, you would say *Budd* on the inbreath and *Ho* on the outbreath. If in doubt, simply use "in-out" or "rising-falling."

So the practice consists of just sitting and noticing whatever sensations, thoughts, and images arise in consciousness, and then gently bringing the attention back to the breath. Keep repeating this process for the duration of the sitting. If necessary, you can set a timer to tell you when the time is up. When the sitting is over, don't jump up and back into your world. Rather, slowly open your eyes, slowly start to move, and slowly move into the world. During this transition, try to be as aware as possible of all sensations, thoughts, and images. Try to maintain a calm and clear mind as long as possible.

From your perspective, there will be good meditation days and bad days, days you seem to make "progress" and days you are frustrated, days you wake up more and days you fall asleep. All of this is secondary to simply continuing the practice. This is very important. You must practice on a regular basis. Your mind will come up with lots of reasons why you can't meditate, today or this week or until....Don't fall for any of these reasons; just do it. And if one of the reasons arises during meditation? Notice it and return to your breath.

With practice, the distinction between when you are meditating and when you are not will gradually dissolve, and a lot of the initial inertia and struggling will be overcome.

Attitude

The attitude you have toward meditation is very important. How you approach it is as important as the form and practice you use. Meditation should be something you regularly do, like brushing your teeth. If you make it into a major task, if you make a big deal out of being a meditator, you may struggle with the practice. So, just do it.

There are three significant and totally interrelated attitudes to cultivate: making friends with yourself, being in the here and now, and letting be.

Making friends with yourself. During meditation, at least at first, you will have many thoughts and reactions about meditation and your ability to meditate. You will evaluate how well you think you are doing and perhaps compare it to how well you think you should be doing or how well you think someone else is doing. You may become dissatisfied by your perceived rate of progress and/or what you are experiencing. You may have some negative feelings toward yourself as a competent meditator. You may tell yourself why meditation is not for you, why this is not the best time in your life for you to be meditating, and so forth.

This type of evaluation is counterproductive, for meditation involves developing a non-evaluative quality of mind. Also, you must begin and be where you are. To assume or desire to be "further" along the path than you are creates delusion and suffering and impairs meditative practice. So during meditation, you need to make friends with yourself, accepting yourself unconditionally. If during meditation you have a pain in your leg you can't ignore, your mind is racing about, and you have thoughts about how poor your meditation practice is going, once again just notice it, and return to noticing your breath. Make friends with yourself. Whatever sensations, images, and thoughts arise are okay, so long as you continue the practice and cultivate unconditionally accepting yourself. You will want to alter your practice based on what you encounter and learn, but always accept yourself.

Being in the here and now. In the early stages of meditation your mind will run all over, including going to plans and anticipations of the future and memories of the past. Meditation practice involves continually coming back to the direct experience of your breathing here and now. With experience, you will see that your mind spends little time in the here and now and a lot of time in the imaginary past and future. During meditation let the past and future go (you can tend to them later). You want to cultivate the ability to simply be here and now.

The purpose of singing is not to get to the end of the song. The purpose of dancing is not to get across the dance floor. Rather, the singing and dancing are enjoyed for the activity itself. A similar attitude should be taken toward meditation. Although meditation practice can lead to many positive results, during meditation one should not be concerned with progress or any possible outcome. Rather, one should simply enjoy the practice and whatever is going on here and now. Like dancing and singing, enjoy the activity of meditation and have a good time. Take meditation instant by instant. Regardless of what happened an instant before, each instant is an opportunity to pull into the here and now. Each instant is an opportunity to relax, center, and be more aware.

Letting be. During meditation you want to let things be as they are and perceive them as clearly as possible. You want to simply be in the here and now, not involved in some struggle or quest. You want to be open to new experiences, but not seek them out. You want to have the attitude that nothing need be accomplished. This is very hard for Americans who often have the feeling they are wasting time if they are not actively trying to achieve something. But this achievement attitude is not what is wanted in meditation. Meditation is a time to simply settle in the here and now and let things be as they are. This is true even for active meditation practices, such as the cultivation of concentration or mindfulness.

Finally, it is important to note that these attitudes of meditation apply to many aspects of living and spiritual practice in general (see appendix). But they are often harder to notice and work

43

with when one is caught up in a complex situation in the melodrama of life. Thus, one begins working with them in the simple situation of meditation, gradually training the mind to notice them in more complex situations. Meditation practice is a microcosm for living in general. For example, learning to make friends with yourself during meditation will lead to your recognizing the importance of doing so at other times.

Meditation is a very simple and very powerful practice for personal and transpersonal growth. But just reading about it is of little value. One must do it regularly for some time. The results can be dramatic, but they often come slowly and subtly. Patience and practice are highly rewarded.

7

Concentration

When most people are awake in the world, their minds are continually running—think, think, see, see, feel, feel, see, think, feel, hear, think, think, see, and on and on. Even when they relax, such as turning to reading or television, it is just a change in the stuff the mind responds to—see, see, think, see, think, think, etc. The mind is a wonderful power tool that is usually running out of control. Since this is the "normal" state of affairs, most people are not aware that their minds are out of control or how advantageous it would be to have more control over this power tool.

In Eastern analogies the mind is described as a drunken monkey, which runs wildly about in a room with six windows. Five windows correspond to the five physical senses (seeing, hearing, etc.), and the sixth window corresponds to the mental sense (thinking, remembering, etc.). The drunken monkey races from one window to the next. For most people it is almost impossible to slow the monkey down or keep it at any particular window for more than a very brief time. This chapter deals with taming the monkey. But the monkey does not want to be tamed and will give us various reasons and experiences to keep from being tamed. And since the monkey is our own mind, these will be convincing reasons and distracting experiences.

There are many impairments caused by a mind out of control. Most people are not very good at listening to others, even though they think they are. When another person is talking and one should be listening, the mind is running about reacting to what is being said and planning what to say in response. As the topic becomes more important and/or emotional, the listening usually decreases. Similarly, many people have trouble reading or studying as the monkey keeps running off. Do you periodically get to the bottom of a page and realize you don't know what you have just "read"?

Some people can't leave their work at the office. When they are at home with the family, their minds keep returning to the business. Some people have trouble getting to sleep at night because their minds keep going to personal concerns, plans for the next day, and so forth. And some are readily thrown into depression because they can't prevent their minds from thinking certain thoughts that lead to depression.

These and many other problems are caused by the drunken monkey. The solution is to tame the monkey through developing concentration or one-pointedness. Concentration is the ability to hold the mind where we want without it running off. Even developing a small amount of concentration can be a big help.

Meditation practices to develop concentration are also called tranquility meditations. For as we develop concentration, we also quiet and relax the mind, which to some extent relaxes the body. Developing concentration is a good way to learn to relax, particularly if many of the sources of stress and anxiety are primarily mental.

From a transpersonal standpoint, there are even stronger reasons for developing concentration. If we are always lost in monkey business, then all we will ever know are our own thoughts and perceptions. Our reality is defined by the monkey. To wake up from the dream, we need to quiet the mind so we can be open to a broader reality and other types of knowing. The door to the transpersonal is found in the spaces between thoughts. Behind and before all the thoughts and perceptions is a domain of consciousness that is very sane and calm. Don Juan, Castaneda's Yaqui Indian sorcerer, said, "The world of sorcerers opens up after the warrior has learned to shut off internal dialogue." The Third Chinese Patriarch of Zen stated, "Stop talking and thinking and there is nothing you will not be able to know." And mystics have continually said that the way to the mystical level requires emptying the mind of all thoughts, images, and perceptions.

Now this does not involve impairing the useful functioning of the mind. (Did your drunken monkey tell you it would?) In fact, getting control of your mind lets you use it more effectively. You control what your mind does and doesn't pursue. But as you quiet the mind, you get free from it, stand back from it, and see it in a broader perspective. Then as your reality is no longer totally restricted to the usual mind stuff, your consciousness is open to a broader and more fundamental reality. You are open to insights and knowledge different from the conceptual knowledge of the monkey.

But this is all much further down the road. At the beginning, you want to develop concentration for its many personal benefits. As your concentration improves, it will aid many other aspects of your spiritual practice, and as your mind quiets, you will gradually have access to the transpersonal domain.

For most people, meditation is the best place to start developing concentration. This is particularly true for people who lead a complex life, such as most Americans. The practices outlined here assume you have spent some time, at least a couple of weeks, doing meditation as described in the previous chapter.

Each time the monkey runs off, gently and firmly reel it back in. In meditation whenever the mind leaves the breath (or other focus of meditation), gently and firmly bring your attention back to the breath, thus gradually developing concentration. You want to notice whatever catches your attention, but minimize getting lost in it. For example, if a particular sound draws your attention, notice the sound, but don't get into categorizing, evaluating, or thinking about the sound. Just notice it and return to your breath. Often you will get lost in the distraction, such as lost in memories or lost in thinking about some feeling. When you become aware that you are lost in some distraction, gently and firmly return your attention to your breath. Don't worry about how long you were lost or judge yourself. Just return to your breath. Forget about the past. Develop concentration here and now in each instant of meditation that you can.

For a while your mind will be readily distracted, regardless of how you structure the meditation. If it is not one thing, it will be another until you have developed some degree of concentration. So, if one day you are particularly distracted by certain sounds, you may wish to reduce these sounds. But don't blame your lack of concentration on the sounds. Even if you eliminate the sounds, something else will distract you. The problem is in the control of your mind.

Sometimes a particular distraction, such as a sound or feeling, is so strong that it keeps pulling your mind to itself. In this situation, focus on the distraction and keep bringing your attention back to it. After the distraction has lost much of its power over your mind, return to your breath as the focus of attention.

At first, most people have a lot of trouble concentrating and are surprised at how little control they have over their minds. Even after one has developed a fairly concentrated meditation, the next day the drunken monkey may be at its wildest. Be patient and accept where you are. Gradually, you will develop concentration during meditation, and you will notice increased concentration in daily living. These effects will probably be subtle at first, but will grow stronger, and after a few weeks you may notice that you concentrate better on your reading and/or listen better when others are talking.

As your concentration improves, you can further develop it in almost any situation. For example, when listening to others or to music, keep your attention on what you are hearing. Whenever you are aware your attention has drifted, gently and firmly bring it back to listening. This type of concentration practice can be done when watching a movie (focus on seeing), exercising (focus on body sensations), bathing (smells and feelings), eating (tastes and smells), praying (absorption in devotion and communion), or almost any other activity.

Concentration helps brings you more into the here and now, and allows you to stop and smell the flowers, to experience the beauty of reality in the midst of monkey business. In a popular story told by the Buddha, a man crossing a field encounters a tiger. Chased by the tiger, the man comes to a precipice, grabs a vine, and hangs over the edge. Hanging there, he sees the tiger above him, and far below a second tiger waiting. Two mice, one white and one black, begin to gnaw on the vine. Seeing a strawberry nearby, the man reaches over with one hand and plucks it. How sweet it tastes!

The Buddhist/yogic literature describes eight *jhanas,* levels of *samadhi* (concentration and absorption) that can be achieved by advanced meditators. During the first four jhanas, concentration continually increases while distractions (including thoughts and pain) decrease. Rapture and bliss are experienced, but are gradually replaced by equanimity, in which all arisings in consciousness are accepted equally. At this point (the fourth jhana), there is no suffering or joy, and concentration is imperturbable. The last four jhanas are beyond all perception of form and involve consciousness of infinite space, objectless infinite consciousness, awareness of no-thing-ness, and finally, neither-perception-nor-nonperception.

Such meditative levels need not concern us now, nor should they be taken as necessary for optimal spiritual work. Rather, seek to gradually increase your concentration and discover how it aids your personal and transpersonal growth.

8

Mindfulness

Everyone has some degree of awareness, a subjective conscious experience of noticing. Not only do the eyes and the brain process visual information, but we often have the subjective experience of seeing something. The object of awareness and awareness itself usually arise together, at the same time, so awareness and the objects of awareness are often confused. But it is possible to develop this awareness over and above what you are aware of. You can increase the range of your consciousness, developing an intentional awareness that Buddhists call "mindfulness."

Developing mindfulness involves cultivating awareness of whatever arises in consciousness. Mindfulness is sometimes called "bare attention" because it is just noticing whatever arises in consciousness. Mindfulness is not thinking about or reacting to what arises; the mind does the thinking and reacting. Mindfulness is just noticing whatever arises in consciousness, including the thoughts and reactions of the mind. Mindfulness is sometimes called "choiceless awareness" because it does not direct or influence what comes into consciousness. It is an open, clear, calm, sane awareness that objectively notices whatever arises in consciousness without elaborating on it, reacting to it, identifying with it, or getting lost in it.

In intermediate stages of developing mindfulness, one moves into the "witness" space. From this vantage point, one observes the contents of consciousness, including thoughts and images, without getting pulled into them. Here one's sense of self is no longer identified with the contents of the mind. This is very liberating and opens the door to the transpersonal.

Many people at first confuse mindfulness with thinking. Thus, a person may have a thought and then think about having the thought. But this is not mindfulness; it is just more thinking. Mindfulness is the awareness of the thought and the awareness of the thinking about the thought. But it is not the thinking itself. It takes a while for many people to distinguish thinking and mindfulness.

Developing mindfulness is helpful at all four levels of being. For example, many people are out of touch with their bodies and do not notice various stresses and strains or the physiological and psychological effects of different foods. As we become more mindful of our bodies, we are able to treat them better and improve our health. Most of us are not very aware of our own behavior, of the subtle interplay among thoughts, feelings, and actions. As we become more mindful of our behavior, we can more readily produce the changes we want and become more effective personally and socially. Developing mindfulness decreases accidents, forgetting, and the need for double-checking.

So developing mindfulness includes expanding our range of awareness. As we increase mindfulness, we can become aware of our behavior earlier in the chain of events and gain greater self-control. Consider a person who suddenly becomes angry. It may be difficult to get out of the anger and open the heart because the anger has already built up a strong force. But through mindfulness training the person can become aware of precursors of anger earlier in the behavioral chain of events, perhaps when the body starts to tense up or the mind starts to generate anger-related thoughts. At this early stage it is easier to stop the anger, thus allowing greater self-control and freedom. Prior to many actions is the intention to act. The average person is seldom aware of this, and just acts; the person who is mindful at the level of intention has more choices. The same is true of feelings, thoughts, and perceptions. Thus, the mindful person has considerably more choice in how she perceives and responds to the world.

For many people the best place to begin developing mindfulness is during meditation. The instructions here assume that you have spent at least a few weeks meditating. Also, for many people, it is best to have developed a certain degree of concentration before emphasizing mindfulness during meditation.

Here is what to do. Sit in meditation (or lie down if that is your form). Put your attention on your breath and quiet your mind with your concentration practice. Then simply let your mind go where it will and notice whatever comes into consciousness. If a sound attracts your attention, notice the sound. You don't direct your mind; this is choiceless awareness. It is important that you merely notice what arises and not get pulled out of bare attention into elaborations or reactions to what arises. If the mind thinks about something, notice the thinking but don't get lost in

55

thought. Try to be mindful and cultivate the witness space. Let your mind and attention go where they will. But whenever there is a gap or pause, bring your attention back to your breath. And all the time try to just notice what arises in consciousness. Sometimes you will be mindful and sometimes you will get lost in the specific contents of consciousness. Gradually encourage the mindfulness, accepting yourself where you are. Like all of our meditation practices, this is slow and subtle, yet very powerful.

If during meditation you need to move your legs, scratch, swallow, cough, or anything else, then do it mindfully. Do it slowly if possible, noticing all intentions, sensations of movement, and other feelings. Notice the rising and falling of your abdomen during breathing. This is often an appropriate point at which to follow the breathing during mindfulness meditation.

In the same way that saying "in-out" or "rising-falling" may help you to follow your breath, so other labeling may help develop mindfulness. If your attention is pulled to a sound, external or mental, then say "hearing." If your attention is pulled to a body sensation, say "feeling"; if a visual image, say "seeing." Say this silently to yourself, not out loud. Eventually, this labeling becomes very subtle, a whisper at the edge of your consciousness. The labeling is an aid to active noticing, a tool to encourage mindfulness.

At first there are only six labels: hearing, seeing, feeling, smelling, tasting, and thinking. "Thinking" includes mental activity such as remembering, planning, evaluating, worrying, and so forth. These six labels correspond to the six windows of the drunken monkey's room. Thus, the labeling during part of a meditation practice might go "thinking, thinking, hearing, thinking, feeling, feeling, feeling, thinking, ..."

As you get more proficient at this use of labels, you can add others such as "moving," "swallowing," "bending," and "scratching." You can use labels for types of thinking, like "planning," "remembering," "judging," and "wanting." Eventually start to notice "intending." Add those labels that are useful to you. But don't get caught up in the process of labeling; this will lead to thinking, not mindfulness.

In this chapter and the previous one, we have seen two major components of meditation—concentration and mindfulness. In concentration meditation we emphasize continually bringing the attention back to a particular object, such as the breathing. In mindfulness meditation we let the mind go more freely and emphasize noticing whatever arises in consciousness, perhaps with the use of labeling. In fact, both forms of meditation contain both components; it is a matter of emphasis. In both forms we want to notice what catches our attention (mindfulness) and develop moment-to-moment one-pointedness (concentration).

With experience you will learn how to find the optimal balance of concentration and mindfulness for any particular meditation session. Sometimes your mind will be scattered and upset and you will want to emphasize concentration; sometimes you will be more tranquil and will want to emphasize mindfulness. But you will always want to be mindful of both components and to develop both to some extent, even when emphasizing one over the other.

One thing is important to keep in mind at all times in meditation: no matter what arises in consciousness, treat it as a distraction and just notice it. If it tends to pull you into it, then gently and firmly return to your breath. Various feelings, images, and insights will arise during meditation. And some of these, after meditation, will be of great interest or value to you, perhaps even changing your life in an important way. This is fine *after* meditation. But *during* meditation, treat *everything* that arises as just something to notice and leave. Don't let the drunken monkey disrupt your meditation.

After some experience with sitting meditation, you may wish to add walking meditation. For this you need a length of space, about ten to fifteen yards long. Clasp your hands lightly in front or behind, and keep your eyes open and looking down about three feet in front of you. Slowly walk back and forth along your path. Too slow is better than too fast. With each step, slowly lift your leg, slowly move it forward, and slowly place it down. The mindfulness labeling for these three components of each step are "lifting," "moving," and "placing." Concentration is developed during walking meditation by continually bringing the mind back to the direct experience of walking. Mindfulness is cultivated by noticing subtler and subtler aspects of the physical sensations of walking and related mental events. When slowly turning around at the end of the path, one can be mindful of "stopping," "turning," "standing," and "intending."

Almost everything said earlier about meditation in general applies to walking meditation. For example, you should start doing it for about ten minutes and gradually build up. And the attitude toward meditation is important. Doing a walking meditation before and/or after a sitting meditation can be very effective. Sometimes you may prefer to do only a walking meditation. In Buddhist meditation intensives where people meditate for many hours a day, the practice consists of alternating between sitting and walking.

After you have developed some degree of mindfulness during meditation, you can start cultivating mindfulness while doing almost anything, including gardening, taking out the garbage, or talking. What you do is put your full attention (concentration) on the activity itself (do it slowly if practical), and notice in detail all the various sensations and thoughts involved. Try to experience all sensations as if they were totally new to you, as if you had never done the activity before, or as if you had just been given vision or hearing.

For example, listen to music as if you had never heard anything before. Exactly what do you experience? Where do you experience it? Eat something very slowly and mindfully. Notice in detail all the changing smells, tastes, and movements of tongue and jaws. Slowly do neck rolls, rotating your head from front to side to back to other side to front. Notice in detail the various sounds and feelings. Notice how relaxed or tense various muscles are. Slowly move some part of your body, such as a finger, and notice in detail the intention to move, the sense of will, and the subtle sensations of movement. When bathing, notice in subtle detail the wide range of feelings, smells, sights, and sounds. Try mindfully doing many different things, such as looking at a friend, seeing yourself in a mirror, reading, visualizing, and thinking.

Eventually you will come to realize that *anything* you do is an opportunity to cultivate more mindfulness. A Zen story tells of the student who visited his master on a rainy day, leaving his shoes and umbrella in the vestibule. The master asked him whether his umbrella was to the left or right of the shoes. Not knowing, the student realized he had much more work to do in developing continual mindfulness.

Try to spend parts of every day increasing mindfulness. After you have been doing this for a while, periodically set aside a day in which you try to be as mindful as possible throughout the whole day. Don't do anything just to get it done. Rather, pull into the here and now of doing the task and *enjoy* the activity itself, regardless of what it accomplishes. Try to do everything slowly, precisely, reverently, and mindfully.

Whatever we do can be done more mindfully and thus is usually done better. The Buddha considered the development of mindfulness of prime importance, often more important than anything else. He described four foundations of mindfulness, four domains where mindfulness can be developed. These are mindfulness of body, feelings, mind, and mental factors.

Mindfulness of body includes being aware of position, such as when sitting or standing, and of movement, as in the walking meditation. Also included is mindfulness of breathing, both during meditation and at other times. Is the breathing long or short, fast or slow, obstructed or smooth?

Women might cultivate being more mindful of their menstrual cycle, including experiences of ovulation and the effects of different aspects of the cycle, such as changes of energy level, mood, and whether one is inner or outer directed.

Mindfulness of feelings involves developing greater awareness of stresses, pains, and degree of relaxation. It involves noticing that we tend to classify all feelings immediately as pleasant, unpleasant, or neutral. It involves noticing later effects of the feeling, such as movement toward or away, and tendencies toward specific emotions, such as anger or sexual arousal.

Mindfulness of mind includes noticing how concentrated and mindful the mind is. It involves becoming aware of how affected the mind is by passion, hatred, confusion, and distraction.

Mindfulness of mental factors involves developing awareness of those aspects of the mind that aid or impair spiritual awakening, such as many of the processes discussed in this book. The Buddha included many things in this foundation of mindfulness. One example is mindfulness of the five hindrances—sense desire (lust), hatred or anger, sloth and torpor, restlessness and worry, and doubt.

Most meditation traditions emphasize concentration/absorption over mindfulness. Buddhism's great contribution is the emphasis given to mindfulness, particularly as practiced in the Theravadin (Hinayana) branch of Buddhism. Within the Theravadin tradition are the highly developed vipassana (insight) meditations. Vipassana practices include a carefully detailed sequence of mindfulness meditations that leads to ever subtler aspects of consciousness. This reveals insights into the fundamental nature of one's self and existence in general (e.g., impermanence, suffering, and egolessness). Beyond this, the practices lead to the ultimate spiritual awakening, including various levels of enlightenment.

9

Opening the Heart

Opening the heart is based on opening oneself
to people and experiences and accepting reality as
it is. It involves gradually transcending the limitations, attachments, and biases of the normally restricted ego-based perspective. Opening the heart
involves the cultivation of unconditional acceptance of reality, as opposed to the usual judging,
rejecting, and fighting with reality. Unconditional
acceptance does not mean becoming passive and
not trying to change anything (the world, other
people, yourself). Your analytic mind will still
evaluate reality and plan courses of action. But
your heart will gradually accept everything at
each step along the way. In fact, your mind will
make more effective decisions when it is less impaired by emotion-backed attachments, and when
it is less thrown off by emotional upset caused by
differences between reality and models of how
reality "should" be.

Meditation is a time to practice opening the
heart. You need only to be open to perceiving
reality as it is in the moment-to-moment here and
now. When meditating, one wants to develop an
openness to the experiences and insights of one's
own being.

Opening the heart also involves opening to experiencing and accepting the whole world and all

people. It involves opening your whole being to what you perceive and how you respond to it. It is based on a relaxed receptivity to other people and situations. The heart opens with unconditional acceptance, even while you are doing things to alter reality.

Opening the heart involves letting other people into your heart and unconditionally accepting them. It often takes great courage to let others into your heart and open yourself to being touched in the heart. Thus, opening to others often involves opening and closing, expanding and contracting, as you gradually work in this area. It is important to remember that accepting or loving another person does not mean that you like that person's behavior; you may try to change another's behavior, or you may avoid that person. But by opening your heart, you learn to unconditionally accept a person over and beyond any of your reactions to particular behaviors. A parent may love a child very much no matter what the child does, while simultaneously disliking some of the child's behaviors and trying to change them. It is important for children and others to know that they are continually loved, even when there are conflicts.

As a general rule, we are all doing the best we can, given our level of understanding, values, experiences, skills, and so forth. Everyone is to be accepted and valued beyond the melodrama of the game or dream. Even when a person acts cruelly or aggressively we need to realize that it is often out of fear or anxiety. So we try to have compassion for the person, not get pulled into a fight, and still do the best thing to encourage more appropriate behavior.

The early Greeks distinguished three different types of love: *eros, philia,* and *agape.* Eros is love primarily based on desire. Philia is based on friendship, brotherly love. And agape is selfless love concerned with the welfare of others. From a transpersonal point of view, eros is a perfectly natural part of being human and is thus respected. Sexual relations can also be the form for powerful *tantric* spiritual practices, although many people use *tantra* as an excuse for hedonism. But in terms of spiritual progress, we don't want the love of opening the heart to be limited to or held back by eros. Eros is usually too tied up in the attachments of the first three centers of consciousness *(chakras)*—which are involved with security, sensation, and power. Eros is often caught in the "more is never enough trap," inviting a never-ending quest for ever more sexual experiences, sensations, conquests, etc.

Opening the heart involves transcending all this and moving to the fourth center of consciousness, the heart chakra. The heart chakra is the transition between the lower levels of humanness and the upper transpersonal levels. The need for love is fundamental and is not satisfied by the stuff of attachments (sex, power, drugs, money, etc.). It is satisfied only by opening the heart.

Transpersonal practice involves assuming and acting from the position of philia, brotherly love, and moving toward agape, selfless love. Selfless love implies getting beyond the self.

Learning to love another, in the broadest sense of the word, includes developing unconditional acceptance, unconditional positive regard, patience, and forgiveness. It involves creating space and support for the other person to learn and grow. Often when with another, it involves being totally with that person in the here and now. Relationships with others should be simple and direct. Don't cloud the relationship with unnecessary heaviness, complexities, expectations, or psychological interpretations. Relax into the relationship and enjoy it and learn from it.

Close relationships usually involve sharing of thoughts, feelings, concerns, goals, insights, touch, conscious spaces, and spiritual movement. Thomas Merton suggested that "infinite sharing is the law of God's inner life."

A common trap is confusing the form of a person's behavior with the essence of how loving the person is. A person who becomes more loving does not necessarily act in any particular way. Similarly, just because a person hugs more or uses the word "love" more often does not mean the person's heart is more open. Of course, as a person learns to love more, it will influence behavior, but not necessarily in stereotypical ways.

To open your heart maximally and learn to love others unconditionally, you must also learn to love yourself unconditionally. For many people this is much harder than loving others. Many people are kinder to their friends than they are to themselves. Most people need to make better friends with themselves and learn to accept themselves unconditionally. Loving yourself does not mean you have to like all your behaviors. There may be things you do or don't do that you want to change. But all the while that you make such decisions and work on such changes, you should unconditionally love and accept yourself as you are. You must be patient with yourself and perhaps forgive yourself. If you argue that it is difficult or impossible to love yourself, then simply love yourself as a person who has trouble loving himself. There is no way out.

In Buddhism a popular meditation for opening the heart is the lovingkindness (metta) meditation. To do this, assume your meditation form and quiet your mind. Then call up images that put you in a loving mood, and let your heart open. These might be images of a loved one, a spiritual teacher or ideal, and/or a nature scene. Keeping the mind quiet and the heart open, shift your contemplation to someone you basically like or love. Start with yourself if possible, then move to someone who has been good to you, such as a benefactor. Let your heart open to this person. You might say to yourself phrases such as "May . . . . be free from danger. May . . . . be free from mental suffering. May . . . . be free from physical suffering. May . . . have the ease of well-being." Then in this meditation and future meditations gradually contemplate people you like or love less and less. With patience and practice you will eventually be able during meditation to open your heart to people you previously did not like. You can learn to love them even though you don't like many of their behaviors. Learning to love one's enemies is a goal of true Christian practices.

By definition the transpersonal domain is entered by getting beyond (trans) the self (the personal level). One practice to facilitate this is selfless service, giving help to others merely for the sake of service. One works toward self-surrender in the here-and-now act of service. This is a critical part of karma yoga, the yoga of service. Selfless giving and serving may involve letting go of one's ego-based attachments in favor of helping another person. In a relationship one can learn not only to give selfess love but also to receive selfless love. For love is often optimal when it is given and received selflessly. At first it may seem that love requires preferring the happiness and welfare of the loved one over one's own. But eventually one realizes that at another level there is no difference.

In the spiritual awakening of the world, as reflected in religion, the period 550-450 B.C. was very significant. In India there were Mahavira, the reformer of the Jain religion, and Siddhartha Gautama, the father of Buddhism and reformer of yoga and Brahminism. In China were Confucius and Lao Tsu, the latter the father of Taoism. The religion of Yahweh was coming together as the world religion of Judaism. It was the beginning of the Golden Age of Greece, which would later strongly influence Western religious thought.

Then came the opening of the world's heart, the emphasis on love in religion. The next 500 years brought the rise, spread, and culmination of the *bhakti* force. Arising in India, bhakti yoga developed as the spiritual path that emphasized love, devotion, and worship. Filling the needs of many people, bhakti yoga became very popular, and dramatically influenced Buddhism. Early Buddhist practices (Theravadin/Hinayana) stressed a simple but difficult path that required much of the practitioner, such as developing concentration and mindfulness in meditation. Although this is a powerful path, it was too difficult for and/or did not suit many people. This led to the development of Mahayana Buddhism, which gives a much greater role to devotion and faith. A classic example of selfless service is the Bodhisattva vow of Mahayana Buddhism. Here the practitioner vows to postpone his own enlightenment until all others become enlightened. In some Buddhist traditions the practitioner begins with Theravadin practices and later adds Mahayana practices.

Christianity arose as the bhakti force culminated. During the time of early Christianity, Eastern spiritual teachers were coming to the Mediterranean and people from the Middle East were going East. Christianity, as taught by its founder Jesus the Christ, is a religion of love and devotion. Unfortunately, Christianity got tied into Western philosophy and politics, and Western history is filled with atrocities committed in the name of Christianity (e.g., the Inquisition, witch hunts, aspects of the Crusades, religious intolerance). By contrast, no major war has ever been fought in the name of Buddhism.

Bhatki yoga, Mahayana Buddhism, and Christianity, in their purest forms, all encourage the opening of the heart through selfless service, unconditional love, and devotion. Many people have a need for some type of devotion or worship, but have trouble relating to the transpersonal. Thus, the religious aspect of these three spiritual paths provides spiritual teachers, manifestations of God, and other religious forms for people to worship and love. In some religious beliefs it is held that God manifests in human form to facilitate spiritual progress. Hindus suggest this has happened many times. Christians believe it has happened once. Opening the heart appropriately can lead to loving many others and to love that goes beyond forms. A powerful bhakti teacher is one who fully realizes in what way she or he is one with God and in what ways not.

Opening the heart is a fundamental and critical part of the universal spiritual path. It can be cultivated within a religious context, but it need not be. Opening the heart will increase happiness, improve interpersonal relations, and lead to transpersonal domains.

10

Reducing Attachments

There is a strong tendency of the mind to grasp at and cling to certain objects of consciousness. Of the myriad of perceptions, images, and thoughts that arise in consciousness, the mind will hang on to some at the expense of others. Thus, the mind will become attached to certain sensations, rituals, expectancies, images of the self, and models of reality.

These attachments are limiting forces, biases in consciousness, and barriers to personal and trans-personal growth. When the mind clings to certain perceptions, it misses and/or distorts others. When the mind is attached to a particular image of self, it distorts information which doesn't fit the image, it restricts changes in the self, and it impairs getting beyond the self.

An attachment often has an emotional component. Ken Keyes, a currently popular teacher, has defined an attachment (he uses the word "addiction") as an emotion-backed demand, expectation, or model that makes you upset or unhappy if it is not satisfied. If I am attached to your acting in a particular way and then you don't act that way, I may get upset and be unhappy. Instead of unconditionally accepting you as you are and, perhaps, trying to influence your behavior, I unnecessarily get upset because reality did not match my model

of how reality was supposed to be. Thus, reducing attachments is a way to gradually increase happiness and peace of mind.

In this chapter is a survey of basic knowledge about causes of attachments, some types of attachments, and ways to reduce attachments. Attachments arise thoughout the day, so they provide a lot of opportunity to work on oneself. Many attachments are quite evident and relate to personal and interpersonal problems. Other attachments, to be discovered later, are very subtle and deal with one's sense of self and how one constructs one's "reality."

Four Noble Truths

Fundamental to Buddhist understanding and practice are the Four Noble Truths, described by the Buddha in his first sermon after his enlightenment. The first Noble Truth is that life is filled with *dukkha*, meaning unsatisfactoriness or suffering. The word *dukkha* is applied to an axle which is off center or a bone out of joint. In Buddhism, dukkha doesn't refer to physical pain so much as to psychological/spiritual unsatisfactoriness. It includes such experiences as the feeling that things aren't quite right, the sense that real happiness is still out of reach, and the conviction that one can't get free. Dukkha is often part of the motivation that drives people to religion, spirituality, science, psychology, and other possible "cures."

The second Noble Truth is that the cause of dukkha is craving. It is the clinging of the mind, the forming of attachments, that causes suffering, not the object of craving itself. For example, money in itself is neither good nor bad nor a cause of dukkha. Doing appropriate things to acquire money to maintain an appropriate life style is often a necessity and can be done spiritually. But to crave money, to be attached to money, causes dukkha. The attached person might think too much of money, be too concerned with getting more money (more is never enough), be anxious about losing it, seek happiness through money, and overlook many more important things.

One reason that craving causes dukkha is that everything is impermanent, everything changes. If you become attached to your youth, a favorite vacation spot, a specific relationship, the nature of your work place, or your life image, then you will probably suffer. Because all of these will change, you will be upset when they are no longer as they were or as you want them to be. The attachments make you less flexible, decrease your happiness, and make you less effective in dealing with and influencing the changes.

If reality does not match your model or expectation of how it should be, then this can be good information and motivate you to accept reality unconditionally and, perhaps, to try to alter reality in a way you see as desirable. But if you cling to your model or expectation and let the discrepancy with reality upset you, then you are suffering unnecessarily and impairing your effectiveness.

The third Noble Truth is that dukkha ends when craving ceases. As one gets free from attachments, suffering decreases. The totally free person suffers no dukkha, lives fully in the here and now, and is joyful, peaceful, and compassionate. This doesn't mean that the person no longer plays the game of life; on the contrary, he plays it more fully and more effectively. Before his enlightenment, the Buddha chopped wood and carried water. After his enlightenment, he chopped wood and carried water. The person free of dukkha is not apathetic, unmotivated, or non-compassionate. The opposite is true. But the person free of dukkha has awakened from the dream.

The fourth Noble Truth is that the way to end craving and dukkha is the Eight-fold Path (see appendix). This includes understanding the psycho-spiritual problem of craving, seeing how the teachings relate to it, and resolving to do something about it. The Eight-fold Path also requires ordering one's life along moral and practical guidelines and developing concentration and mindfulness. It involves consciously doing things that are harmonious and in balance.

In Buddhism there are four kinds of clinging: to sensual attachments, to views and opinions, to rites and rituals, and to an idea of selfhood. There are three kinds of desires: sensual desire, desire for becoming, and desire not to become (not be this or that). And there are three defilements of the mind: hatred, greed, and lust.

Chakras

In yogic philosophy it is suggested that there are seven centers of consciousness called *chakras*. The word "chakra" means "wheel" in Sanskrit. A chakra is a center of interaction of consciousness, mind, body, and energy. The seven chakras correspond to seven areas of the body—anal, genital, navel, heart, throat, "third eye" (between eyes and above eyebrows), and crown (top of head). It is suggested that during psycho-spiritual progress, a basic spiritual force called *kundalini* arises through the chakras and may undo some of the knots and attachments associated with the chakras. The arising of kundalini is often a byproduct of various spiritual practices. But some practices (e.g., *siddha yoga*) are aimed at directly influencing the kundalini.

According to contemporary interpretation, each chakra corresponds to a particular category of attachments. The anal chakra corresponds to security attachments. Here we find fear, worry, and paranoia about such things as possessions, home, relationships, social roles, self-concept, other's opinions of us, and being "wrong." The genital chakra corresponds to sensation attachments. This includes craving for sensory pleasure and greater complexity. It involves fleeing from boredom and sameness. It includes sex in the broadest sense and Freudian dynamics. The navel chakra corresponds to power attachments, including issues of will, domination and submission, socio-political influence, prestige, pride, and energy.

Most people's attachments fall into the three categories of security, sensation, and power. Therefore, the above description is often helpful when you are learning to notice attachments. When you become aware of the results of an attachment, described below, or the dynamics of the attachment itself, then think about how the attachment is based on security, sensation, and/or power. This will help you notice other attachments and the interrelationships among them.

A common trap at this level is the "more is never enough" trap. A person is driven to getting more and more security, sensation, or power. If one is attached to sensual pleasures, then more sensual pleasures seems better. If one is attached to power, then one is driven for more and more power. But if you always want more, you will

77

never be satisfied. More is never enough. This is a tough trap to get out of. It involves realizing enough is enough. It involves realizing that happiness and spiritual progress are not achieved by questing for more. They are achieved by letting go of attachments.

The heart chakra is the transition from the three lower level chakras, which are strongly tied to the physical world, to the three higher level chakras, which are more spiritual. The heart chakra is based on opening the heart, including the development of nurturance, empathy, compassion, and unconditional love. Attachments at this level block the opening of the heart and may lead to irritation or anger.

The throat chakra corresponds to creativity, trust, receptivity, and the ability to receive nurturance and grace from others and from "above." Practices at this level may involve singing, chanting, art and music as devotion, mandalas, dream analysis, and altering reality by altering verbal concepts. The "third eye" chakra corresponds to mindfulness, introspection, intuition, and integration of different kinds of consciousness. And the crown chakra corresponds to enlightenment, the highest state. This is often represented in paintings by a halo over the head.

Yoga as a discipline is intended to lead the practitioner through the lower chakras until the ego is transcended and union with the fundamental ground is achieved. The word "yoga" means "union" or "yoke" to this fundamental ground, pure consciousness, Godhead.

In yoga it is suggested there are five causes of suffering *(klesas)*: lack of awareness of reality, sense of egoism, attraction to persons or objects, repulsion from persons or objects, and strong desire for life.

Effects of Attachments

At first, the easiest way to know the presence of an attachment is by its effects. These effects might include undesired emotions, distorted perception, and/or impaired thinking. First you become more mindful of such effects and trace them back to specific attachments, like security, sensation, or power. Then you gradually cultivate mindfulness so that it occurs earlier and earlier until you are aware of the dynamic processes of the attachments while they are happening. But first let us consider the effects.

When a craving is not satisfied, it often causes an unwanted emotion such as anxiety, anger, or jealousy. This often arises when a model or expectation of how reality should be does not match how reality actually is. Bob plans to spend some time with Jo who cancels at the last minute. Bob is upset because his plans for the evening have fallen apart. He gets mad at Jo and his evening is ruined. Bob's expectation for the evening did not match reality, so he upset himself, ruined his own evening, and blamed his unhappiness on Jo. A less attached Bob would tell Jo whatever is appropriate when she changed the plans and take all of this into account in future dealings with her. But then he would let go of his old plans for the evening and make new plans for an enjoyable and/or profitable evening. The best course to follow when you are thrown off balance, such as when you become angry, is to take responsibility for it, catch yourself, recenter, look for attachments, and let go of any attachments you can.

A second possible effect of an attachment is distortion and/or limiting of perception. A person caught up in sensual attachments may view people of the opposite sex primarily in terms of potential sexual partners. This causes one to overlook or distort many other aspects of the other, such as personality, intelligence, or spirituality. If a woman is friendly to a man just to be friendly, it is often interpreted as a sexual come-on. A person caught up in power attachments tends to perceive others in terms of power. Thus a politician obsessed with personal power will see the world in terms of what increases or threatens that power. Blinded by attachments, the politician overlooks and distorts much that is more important.

Dick worked for the police department and saw a lot of crime. This led to attachments regarding the security of his home and family. One day a carpenter came to Dick's home to give him an estimate for some work to be done. While getting a piece of equipment, the carpenter took a wrong turn in the house and briefly stepped into a side hall. Dick perceived the carpenter as checking out his house for later theft. He then dismissed the carpenter and guarded his home carefully for the next week or so. Making your home secure in appropriate ways does not imply an attachment, but Dick was not acting appropriately. His security attachments caused him to see threats which probably did not exist. This upset him, caused him weeks of worry, and made it much more difficult to find a carpenter.

There is an old story about a person who approaches the gatekeeper of a town and asks what type of people live there. The gatekeeper in turn asks, "What type of people live in the town you came from?" The person answers, "Unpleasant, uncooperative, and unfriendly." The gatekeeper responds: "You will find the same here." Later a second traveler arrives and asks the same question. Again the gatekeeper asks, "What type of people live in the town you came from?" The traveler replies, "Pleasant, helpful, and friendly." The gatekeeper says, "You will find the same here."

Finally, attachments may impair thinking. Students anxious about their performance on a test don't think as clearly as they could. Those who are convinced they cannot understand machines, such as automobiles or computers, will not think as clearly as they otherwise might when the machine breaks down. They will not notice relevant aspects of the machine; they will not apply problem-solving skills they would apply in other situations. Attachments impair creativity and tend to lead to set mental habits and quick "solutions."

Numerous Western psychologies have dealt with these types of effects of attachments. Examples include psychodynamic defenses, cognitive dissonance theory, and perceptual defense and vigilance. But understanding the effects in terms of attachments is more basic and general.

Getting Free

The first step in freeing yourself from attachments is having the right attitude toward them. If you don't like them and wish you didn't have them, then you will have trouble noticing them and working with them. On the other hand, if you take delight in discovering and working with them, it will be much easier. A good attitude is that discovering an attachment is a blessing, because it allows you the opportunity to do some work in freeing yourself and moving in a direction which is easier, happier, more effective, and more spiritual. When an attachment arises, stay in the here-and-now with it, taking full responsibility for your thoughts, feelings, and actions. Cultivate openness, clarity, and unconditional acceptance of attachments. Have a good time doing all of this.

With the right attitude toward attachments, you can practice developing greater and greater awareness of them. Notice common traps such as "more is never enough" or "reality versus model/expectancy." Use classification schemes, such as the chakra system, to help you label and explore attachments.

Another common problem to look for is the tendency to multiply emotions. A person who gets angry at someone may get angry at being "made" angry, thus multiplying the anger. An anxious person may get anxious about being anxious, thus multiplying anxiety. A person in pain may be upset at *feeling* pain, thus increasing the subjective experience of pain. People struggling with personal or spiritual issues often end up struggling with the fact that they are struggling. In all these cases, you will usually want first to stop the multiplying effect and then to deal with the initial emotion or sensation.

Quieting your mind through meditation can help you see attachments and their effects more clearly. It can also help you step back and dissociate from the attachments, making it easier to work with them. Developing mindfulness of attachments and their effects increases your awareness of attachments and increases your mindfulness.

Once you notice an attachment, you have the chance to get free from it. Being free does not mean being apathetic. A common misconception is that being free from attachments is to not care, to be unmotivated, or to have no preferences. This simply is not true. We can be motivated to protect our health without getting caught in security attachments. We can prepare a tasty meal without being driven by sensation attachments. Having goals, preferences, and motives is necessary and appropriate. It is the grasping and clinging to attachments that is limiting and destructive. The free person has unattached motives and preferences. Thus the major work, according to Ken Keyes, is to upgrade attachments to preferences.

Some people who try to get free adopt phony states of happiness, love, or acceptance. Phoniness seldom works in the long run. We must see and accept attachments as they are and do something about them. It is not helpful to pretend the attachments aren't there. It is destructive to pretend you are free when you aren't. It is limiting to think you will optimize love or happiness by acting loving or happy in a superficial way.

When you become aware of an attachment, what should you do? The simple universal answer is just to let go of the attachment. A popular Eastern analogy is that of a monkey trap consisting of a gourd tied to a tree. A hole in the gourd lets the monkey reach inside for food, but is too small to get the food back out. When the monkey grabs the food, its paw is trapped. Now to get free all the monkey has to do is let go; but it won't. All people have to do to get free from an attachment is let go; but they usually don't.

A more practical answer is that when you become aware of an attachment, you should actively do something to stop the undesired chain of behaviors and encourage more desirable behaviors. Sometimes the action to be taken is based on practices outlined in this book, such as quieting the mind or opening the heart. But at first many significant attachments will be at the biological and behavioral levels. Specific actions can be taken for these types of attachments, actions not described in this book. (See my book *Skills of Living* for practices and references.) For example, consider a person addicted to a drug such as alcohol, nicotine, caffeine, marijuana, or amphetamines. Although some people may be able just to let go of such an attachment, it is usually more effective to engage a comprehensive program of change geared to the particular addiction.

When you notice an attachment, you need to take an action that is appropriate for that attachment. Examples are quieting the mind, stopping unwanted thoughts, saying affirmations, imaging specific scenes, deep breathing, relaxing the body, tightening incompatible muscles, and leaving the situation. For some attachments you may wish to devise a systematic treatment program, while other attachments can be taken on as they arise.

At times you will be fairly free of gross attachments. During these free times develop mindfulness of what it is like to be free. Sometimes gross attachments will take over, things will get out of control, and you will act like a robot. You might be thrown into anger or anxiety you can't control. You might do something you are trying to avoid, such as smoke another cigarette or be too unassertive. During robot time, don't just fall into it and give up. Be mindful of the attachments and their effects. Be mindful of mental justifications for undesired behaviors. Don't multiply emotions. And don't let being a robot now justify being a robot later.

Important working times are those between being free and being a robot. These are the times you can be lazy and let yourself slide into robot. Or you can be a warrior, take responsibility for yourself, apply your change techniques, and move into being free. The more you take advantage of these working times, the more the free times will expand and the robot times will decrease.

Get to know your attachments. Play with them. Develop systematic ways to gradually reduce them. Don't be impatient. Have a good sense of humor about it all. Note the various forms of energy that are often involved. Eventually, you will learn to direct and utilize this energy in profitable ways. Tantric practices, particularly within Tibetan Buddhism, deal with converting energy from attachments into a better form.

Remember when working with attachments that you are not your behaviors, and that includes the behaviors of the mind, such as thoughts and imaginings. Don't identify with your behaviors. See them as accurately as you can and accept them unconditionally. Make friends with yourself. Then change those behaviors that need changing.

The more you get free from attachments, the subtler the attachments get. At first the most obvious and significant attachments are security, sensation, and power attachments related to the material world, interpersonal relationships, and psychological problems. As these types of attachments are eliminated, upgraded to preferences, or transcended, one turns to more subtle attachments related to such things as the nature of self and how one constructs reality. Whereas at the grosser levels the practices outlined in this book may be helpful but insufficient, at the subtler levels these practices can become the primary change approach. The more one moves in a spiritual or transpersonal direction, the more the spiritual practices have an immediate practical application.

One of the last attachments to go is the attachment to being free from attachments. A yogic analogy is of a fire burning up attachments. You use a stick to stir up the fire and keep it going. This stick is the desire to be free. When the fire nears the end, you throw in the stick to burn.

Practice Exercise

Here is a list of attachments I have collected from a group of students. As an exercise, read each attachment and think about how it functions and what effects it produces. How would you work with such an attachment? What attachment of yours is similar in some way?

I get irritated when others are late, but not when I am late. When I am late, I know good reasons for it.

If I have an idea for the perfect music for a situation and others disagree, it upsets me.

I am caught up in self-importance. If I do something foolish in public, I think people pay more attention or care more than they do.

I interrupt others when they are studying, but I don't like to be interrupted myself.

I want others to agree with me, to assume what I assume.

I feel like less of a person if I make a mistake.

I worry before I have any reason to worry: "But what if...."

I often use the strategy of anticipating the worst so I won't be disappointed.

I can't gracefully accept a compliment. I can't believe it or at least I respond as if I don't.

I degrade people with whom I feel in competition.

If I think a person is upset about something I did, then I get mad at him or her.

I don't properly listen to a person who is too fat. A person's appearance affects his or her credibility.

I am holding onto an old gratifying relationship. I have inertia about new relationships or redefining old relationships which may not be as gratifying.

I often need to explain myself.

When talking with my girlfriend on the phone, I get defensive if she says "I have to go now" before I do.

Bad drivers are frustrating to me, particularly slow drivers in the wrong lane.

Every day is filled with attachments that you can practice being mindful of and work at reducing. Reducing attachments will improve your daily living and free you to move toward higher levels of being.

III
Overall Practice

11

Cleaning House

As is made clear in all the major spiritual disciplines, for us to make optimal progress at the personal level and toward the transpersonal, we must first order our life along moral and practical guidelines. We must clean up daily living before we can optimally transcend it. Many people hope that spiritual work will somehow absolve them from the mess they have created in their personal and interpersonal lives. Although there are considerable grace and "miracles" in the game, we will continually get thrown back on unresolved issues and problems. Transpersonal practices may help us see and approach the problems better, but the problems still need to be dealt with at their level.

In terms of our "levels of being" (Chapter 3), we need to resolve issues at the biological level before we can optimally work on the behavioral level. We need to deal with nutrition, exercise, breathing, and drugs to purify, strengthen, and come into greater harmony with the temple of the body. Similarly, we must deal with issues at the behavioral level before we can work optimally at the personal level—including psychological concerns related to thoughts, emotions, interpersonal interactions, and personal skills. We must confront practical issues, such as those related to vocation and social problems. Finally, we must deal with matters at the personal level before we can most effectively move toward the transpersonal. We must resolve problems related to self-concept, self-esteem, and fragmentation of the self.

The transpersonal is always present and available and is not "achievable" by changes at the biological, behavioral, and personal levels. However, by removing problems at these three levels, we clear the way for transpersonal realizations and transformation of being. Zen is filled with stories of "instant enlightenment." But what is not stressed enough in the West is the many years of training the Zen practitioner went through to prepare for the sudden experience of enlightenment.

In a previous book, *Skills of Living*, I summarized many of the practical things we can do to get control over our lives and to clear up problems at the biological, behavioral, and personal levels, with emphasis on the behavioral. I discuss methods such as how to restructure the environment, relax body and mind, get motivated, get organized, alter habits, work with thoughts and images, choose appropriate nutrition and exercise, and deal with many common problems such as fears, weight control, and smoking. With these issues as a basis, in the last part of that book I move into those areas that overlap the domain of this book: personal freedom, happiness, love, inner peace, and mindfulness.

Over and above these specific topics, there are more general themes that run throughout *Skills of Living*. One is the importance of continually developing objective observation of one's feelings, thoughts, and other behaviors. This is accom-

plished through record-keeping and logs, specific exercises, and mindfulness practices. A second general theme is the basic strategy of taking small steps and being committed to a plan of action that often needs to be revised. Finally, there is the importance of cultivating unconditional acceptance of oneself while simultaneously recognizing the desirability of change.

The key here for many people is developing discipline. A person often knows what needs to be done but somehow never seems to have the time or energy to get around to it. The melodrama of daily living has us too tied up. Some convince themselves that discipline is somehow counter to their personality, philosophy of living, or spiritual path. These people are usually greatly impaired in any attempt at self-improvement.

As the spiritual warrior ready to grab hold of our lives and move on, we can recognize the value of precision and discipline in everything we do. We may even do things simply for the sake of developing discipline. Thus we take the things we must do or want to do—like meditation—and simply do them, with precision and awareness and without making a big deal of it. This then gradually leads to more power, freedom, and choice.

In addition to cleaning up our lives in practical and psychological ways, we must also order them along ethical principles. In all the major spiritual disciplines there are general rules of conduct that include avoiding undesired behaviors and encouraging desired behaviors, the two limbs of yoga called *yama* and *niyama* respectively. Thus we have the Ten Commandments of Judaism and Christianity, the various precepts of Buddhism (see appendices), and many other ethical codes that discourage killing, violence, stealing, lying, and greed, and that encourage appropriate respect and devotion.

In the domain of religion, people are told to obey the ethical codes to achieve certain rewards and avoid certain punishments. This might be conceptualized in terms of heaven and hell, karma, or more immediate worldly effects. But as we progress spiritually, ethical behavior becomes more and more natural and obvious, and thus less effortful. The awakened being does not avoid stealing or lying because he is very "good" or because he fears the consequences of stealing and lying. Rather, it simply makes no sense to steal or lie. The awakened or enlightened being is motivated by compassion and a cosmic perspective, not the grasping and clinging that motivates most unethical behavior.

The various ethical codes basically describe the way a spiritually advanced person would normally act. So a good part of a spiritual practice is to adopt such an ethical code as a way to predispose your understanding and progress toward a more advanced position. And changes in overt behavior often lead to changes in thoughts, attitudes, and sense of self.

It is also worthwhile to reflect on the great depth and generality of most ethical injunctions. For example, the yama of yoga includes non-violence. Overt violence is easy to see, but what about the violence in thoughts and subtle mental predispositions toward negative judgments. One of the Judeo-Christian commandments is against coveting, the craving for something not yours.

Dealing with coveting is very difficult and involves subtle cravings and attachments of the mind. And what about stealing? What should not be stolen? What about stealing things, ideas, people's time? What about truthfulness? Do you *always* tell the truth? If not, why not? We can profit from pursuing the practical implications of the ethical principles at increasingly more general and more subtle levels, rather than just trying to follow the principles superficially and understanding them philosophically or religiously.

Finally, it is worth repeating that very many people would do better relative to transpersonal goals if they spent less time thinking and reading about spiritual topics and more time cleaning up and ordering their lives along moral and practical guidelines. This will then facilitate their spiritual progress, which will lead to spiritual insights and understanding. From this more advanced perspective, they will see that many of the philosophical issues that seemed important before are now no longer significant or meaningful.

When the Buddha was asked metaphysical questions, about such matters as previous lives or levels of heaven, he usually told the questioner it is more important to tend to more practical concerns, such as interpersonal and vocational problems.

Of course, all of this interacts with other aspects of transpersonal practice, such as opening the heart, quieting the mind, and reducing attachments. In Buddhism it is said that morality *(sila)*, concentration *(samadhi)*, and insight *(prajna)* all influence each other. An improvement in one leads to improvement in the others. For example, cleaning up ethical issues in one's daily life makes it easier to develop concentration during meditation, for the meditation is less disrupted by ethical concerns and their consequences. And conversely, as you quiet your mind, it is easier to see and work with moral concerns.

12

Readiness to Know

In the domains of personal and transpersonal knowledge, we are continually bombarded by teachings and information. But most people miss most of this because they are not ready to see and hear the teachings. Their attachments limit their ability to perceive and understand those things they want and/or need to know. Often the more basic and important the teaching, the harder it is to hear.

So in personal and transpersonal growth, it is not enough just to seek out information. We also need to cultivate readiness to hear and know the lesson, the truth, the broader perspective, and the fundamental insight. The teachings are ever present. It is a matter of quieting the mind and opening the heart so we can hear and see better. It is a common spiritual maxim that the teacher will appear when the student is ready.

One block to readiness to know is intellectual closed-mindedness. We can get so caught up in a particular set of ideas or forms that we are not open to new experiences and knowledge. We are more interested in defending, justifying, and explaining our own positions. In an oft-told Zen story, a university professor goes to visit the master Nan-in to learn about Zen. While serving tea, Nan-in fills the professor's cup and keeps on

pouring though the cup is overflowing. When the professor finally points this out, Nan-in says, "Like this cup, you are full of your own opinions and speculations. How can I show you Zen unless you first empty your cup?"

Now if what we need to learn is a challenge to our images of self or world, then we often are not ready to hear. We misperceive, lie to ourselves, and have distorted memories rather than seeing and learning something that confronts our sense of self. Bob will have complex reasons for why he is not doing well at work rather than realizing it is his attitude toward his coworkers that is causing the problem. Sue is fearful of developing close relationships with men because whenever she does they end up leaving her. She is not ready to hear how she drives men away in order to maintain her belief about them. Often the problem gets worse and worse as we resist learning. Bob's job situation and Sue's relationships with men both deteriorate and lead to other problems.

All of us have lessons to learn about ourselves and our relationships with others and the world. When we learn the lessons our lives will be easier and happier. But our attachments blind us so that we resist learning. It is as if we get a little bump to point out the lesson, but we don't hear. So we are hit a little harder to point out the lesson again. Still we don't hear. Each time we get hit harder and harder until we finally pay attention and are motivated to hear. It is amazing how hard people can get hit and still not listen.

One can reduce some of the blocks by a change in attitude about self-discovery. Rather than feeling anxious or threatened by what you may learn about yourself, cultivate a positive attitude toward whatever you discover, for the discovery will help you move on. Take delight in discovering attachments, barriers, and assumptions that are limiting your personal and transpersonal growth. Have a good time on the journey.

A problem in hearing spiritual truths is that many of them are so simple and basic that they usually are understood superficially. It is in generality, depth, and subtlety that the power of spiritual truth lies, not in philosophical and conceptual understanding. Intellectual understanding of the Buddha's idea of impermanence is quite different from a direct experience of the impermanence of everything.

Moving toward the spiritual and transpersonal realms is moving in a direction that gets simpler, not more complex. Life gets lighter, not heavier. Spiritual teachings, like ethical principles, are known in many ways other than conceptual knowledge alone. They are best known through direct experience resulting from a continually evolving journey into the nature of one's being and beyond.

As an exercise, consider the next paragraph carefully. It is a commonly held postulate from the Perennial Philosophy, an enduring and fairly universal spiritual perspective. It doesn't matter for the exercise whether the statement is true or false. Simply read and consider it carefully. Note your thoughts and reactions and how they relate to readiness to hear.

The highest spiritual levels cannot be obtained. For if they could, they would be limited in time, occurring after some time, and separable from you, since it is something you obtain. Rather, these higher levels are one without a second, un-

limited, and outside of time and space. Therefore, they are always already here. You are already enlightened, even if "you" don't "realize" it.

Now even if this is true, just reading it will not make it self-evident to most people. They are not able to hear it in a way that transforms them. The practices surveyed in this book help cultivate the readiness to hear and know, even though there is nothing you have to do.

So how can you tell when you are understanding clearly as opposed to being caught in one of your attachments? How can you tell true spiritual insight from tricks of the mind? There are no simple answers to such questions. We must learn for ourselves, making mistakes along the way. As we learn to quiet our minds and open our hearts, we find a fundamental level of sanity prior to all the melodrama. We learn to tune in to the still small voice within. We learn to identify a sense of clarity and obviousness that is part of basic insights. We come to see how such insights alter our perceptions, values, and behaviors.

After the last supper when Jesus was leaving his disciples, they were concerned about what they would do when their teacher was gone. Jesus told them not to worry for he would send the Holy Spirit to be their inner guide.

13

Finding Your Way

When a person decides to pursue a spiritual path, the question is often which path to follow. Sometimes circumstances dictate a particular path. But often one is confronted by a variety of paths with associated stories and promises. Which path to take? What are some general guidelines for making such decisions?

First, it must be realized that finding your way is part of the path itself. Learning how and why you choose different paths is an important part of the overall process. What attachments are involved? What entices you in the spiritual supermarket? Cultivating a readiness to hear and know is important here.

Along the way, you may make many mistakes; this is the norm. But don't be anxious about this or be obsessed with not making mistakes. Everyone makes mistakes and they are wonderful opportunities to learn.

Different paths are right for different people at different times. One's personality, attachments, psychological needs, and readiness to know may lead to a particular path. Of the major world systems, yoga more than any other recognizes the need for different paths (yogas) for people with different needs. For example, there is *hatha* yoga, the yoga best known in the West, which emphasizes working with the body, including postures, breathing, nutrition, and cleansing. There is *karma* yoga, which stresses selfless service, action without attachment, and spiritualizing work in daily life. *Bhakti* yoga is the yoga of love, devotion, and ritual worship. *Jnana* yoga is built on self-analysis, awareness, and discrimination, while *raja* yoga, as codified by Patanjali, includes all of these yogas.

Along with finding your way is the recognition that the path which is right for you is not necessarily right for someone else. Thus, an important part of spiritual practice is developing unconditional respect for the paths of others and the realization that there is much to be learned from people on other paths and with other perspectives. The American Indians' use of the medicine wheel often incorporated this understanding. People with different perspectives and understandings would sit together at the wheel to share their different views. It was understood that the Great Way encompasses all the points of the wheel.

It is often the case that the strength of a particular path is also the cause of many of its problems. For example, one person's path may be largely intellectual, with a lot of reading, thinking, and philosophizing. This can be good to a point, but it can also result in the person being lost in his own conceptual knowledge and not moving into other types of knowing. Or one may be on a devotional path. A common trap here is distorting reality so it takes a form that is easier to love. More important is learning to perceive and love reality as it is.

Another common trap is the difficulty in letting go of a particular method, group, teacher, or path

after its usefulness is past. You may still respect, honor, and value it; but you need to be able to let it go. Say you come to a difficult river that you wish to cross and eventually find a boat that gets you to the other side. You may appreciate the boat, but you need to leave it at the shore and travel on. It would be a mistake to carry the boat on your back because it had helped you. It would also be a mistake to argue that everyone should have a boat like yours, and the only way across the river is the way you came.

Related to this is the more-is-never-enough trap. Because a particular method or teacher has been helpful to you does not mean that more of the same will be more helpful. Realize when you have had enough and move on. Don't be attached to just more of the same.

It is important to follow your path with great precision, willfulness, and skill. You need to give your path the importance it deserves without getting lost in its forms. You need to stay with your path through all its obstacles and not jump from path to path. Yet you need to be able to take a new path when the time has come.

There is an important paradox in the analogy of following a path. That is, the essence of the ultimate spiritual path is not to get you somewhere else at some other time. Rather, it is a matter of being more fully in the here and now. All the practices described in this book are intended to bring you into a more direct experience of reality here and now. It is not an issue of getting "there"; it is an issue of being "here." It is not "then," but "now."

As in dancing, it is not so much where meditation takes you that is important. Rather, it is how you do the activity itself. Where a spiritual path may lead is of secondary importance to the here and now of how you are traveling the path. You need to let go of the past and take responsibility for your current psychological and spiritual state. You need to let go of anticipations of the future and confront the present. Pets can be good teachers in this area, for animals appear to live much more in the here and now than humans.

In fact, you are always only in the here and now. No matter where you go, if you ask where you are, the answer is "here." And no matter when you ask yourself what time it is, the answer is "now." But most people's minds are dominated by memories of the past and plans and fantasies of the future. So they get lost in this imaginary mind stuff and don't recognize the reality of the here and now. However, if one looks closely, it is clear that there is no past, only memories now, and no future, only plans and fantasies now. Spiritual practices bring one more into the here and now. Enlightened persons do not disappear into some cosmic cloud. Instead, they are more fully in the here and now. This does not mean they become irresponsible or no longer plan for the future. They still think and plan appropriately, but do not get lost in the contents of the thoughts and plans.

Finally, the hardest and most subtle teaching in finding our way is the basic fallacy of "seeking" itself. If the highest spiritual levels cannot be obtained and are already always there, then anything which suggests the idea of seeking or obtaining them perpetuates a myth and a dilemma which is a fundamental obstacle. Zen is based on the premise that a person is already free, that the chains are an illusion. We are free as soon as we cease to believe we need to free ourselves. Thus, many contemporary teachers, such as Krishnamurti and Da Free John, have continued to attack the search itself.

But this teaching is very difficult to hear and has not been particularly useful or practical. How do you stop seeking? How do you realize the chains are illusions? So one follows a path until one is ready to really hear, in a way that transforms one's being, that the path was both unnecessary and necessary. Meditation is a good place for many people first to come to grips with being involved in a spiritual practice without trying to obtain anything.

It is important to be able to relax into a spiritual path and not make it unnecessarily unpleasant or heavy. So, follow the path with precision, compassion, and clarity. But relax and enjoy it.

14

Teachers

Most people on a spiritual path can profit from the input of spiritual teachers (gurus), and many spiritual traditions consider this necessary, although many people have done well without one.

There are many ways a teacher can help. In some cases, it is useful to get practical advice from someone who is further along the path. Some teachers act as mirrors and help us see ourselves more accurately and expose our "games." Often we don't like the reflection in the mirror and we blame the mirror. Some teachers can pull the student more into the here and now or into particular conscious spaces. Some teachers can fill one with love or spiritual energy (e.g., *shaktipat*). Some offer themselves as the personification of what they teach, while others are only passing on spiritual information.

Unfortunately, many people who publicly function as spiritual teachers are not very spiritually advanced or are outright frauds, whether they know it or not. There are a lot of power traps in being a public guru, and a teacher who gets caught in such attachments may do more enslaving than freeing of the student. The amount of jealousy, competition, empire-building, and sexual misconduct among major contemporary spiritual teachers is amazing. Few teachers who rise to a position of great power, respect, and adoration seem able to handle it. Thus the most popular teachers are not necessarily the best teachers. On the other hand, among the better known teachers are many legitimate, sincere, powerful, advanced gurus.

As a general rule, a spiritual teacher should be trying to incorporate spiritual ideals and practices into his or her own life. Thus, there should be evidence of such things as a quieting mind, opening heart, and getting free from attachments. One should be suspect of a guru whose personal life and relationships are out of order and causing suffering. Since spiritual progress usually leads to a freer and lighter position, an advanced guru will seldom impose unnecessary heaviness and will often have a sense of humor about the game of life. On the other hand, many spiritual teachers choose to act in outrageous ways to challenge the students' preconceptions about the form spirituality must take.

An enlightened being does not necessarily choose to be a visible public guru or to assume the form that one might expect. Thus, it could be that the bus driver or Aunt Sally might be an awakened being, but most people do not realize them as such because they are not ready to know. Historically, there have been many great gurus that people thought were fools.

In fact, everyone is your guru in that you can learn from everyone. Adopting this perspective toward others can help open the heart. For various reasons, you have more intense relationships with some of these gurus, such as your family and friends. With these people it is important always to recognize the spiritual component. Thus, in

addition to all the other things a marriage relationship is, it also is a tremendous opportunity for two people to help each other and learn from each other on the spiritual path. Your spouse can be your best guru since he or she knows you so well, and since ideally you are merging in being, although not necessarily in personality.

Children are often incredible teachers. A parent can learn much from the clarity and innocence of the child. And the parent has the opportunity to help the child learn and develop in a way that will facilitate later spiritual work. In addition, the drama of the family is an excellent arena for personal and transpersonal learning, from basic behavioral and personal issues to more general concerns such as loyalty and protection.

Many people involved in spiritual work seek and value associating with others with similar interests, perhaps through a church, discussion group, or community. Through such organized meetings people share ideas and discoveries, raise questions, provide support and encouragement to each other, bring in teachers, and initiate various activities. Several of the great spiritual traditions, such as Buddhism, emphasize the value of such a community of spiritually-minded people.

Finally, teachers can occur in many forms including animals, phenomena in nature, guides within consciousness, books, and everything else. When the student is ready, the teacher will appear. The form of the teacher is not as important as the essence of the teaching.

15

Continual Practice

At first, spiritual practice is something one does every now and then, such as going to church once a week, meditating periodically, or working for a charity on some afternoons. There is a sense that there is a real difference between the sacred and the profane.

But as our spiritual practice becomes more sophisticated, these distinctions break down. Everything that we do can be approached spiritually. Taking out the garbage can be as spiritual as doing religious chants in a temple. Washing dishes can be as good an opportunity for spiritual awakening as meditating in the Himalayas. The form of what one does should not be confused with the essence of spirituality.

Associated with this is the practical realization that every instant of one's life is an opportunity to do spiritual work. Every moment is an opportunity for one to do things such as quiet the mind, increase mindfulness, open the heart, or reduce attachments. Every situation is an opportunity to choose to wake up or to stay lost in the dream. At any time and place you can catch yourself, relax, pull into the here and now, and apply one or more of your spiritual practices.

Although disciplined times of formal sitting meditation are important, each day is filled with many opportunities for mini-meditations. A good time for a mini-meditation might be just before others wake up, during a break in work, while sitting in a waiting room, or while waiting for a bus. You don't need to assume a particular form or make a big deal of it. Just close your eyes, put your attention on your breathing, quiet your mind, and increase your awareness. It can be for just a couple of minutes. Even one minute is helpful. Mini-meditations allow you to take time out from the game and recenter yourself. By having a number of mini-meditations throughout the day, you increase your meditation skills and facilitate the development of a meditative stance in daily living. And you loosen your attachments for the moment.

At first, concentration is usually best developed during formal meditation. But with practice we gradually become more and more aware of how focused or one-pointed our minds are in all situations. When listening to a friend or listening to music, we can be aware of how much the mind stays on what we want to hear and how much it runs off to other things, such as sensations, thoughts, and fantasies. We can then apply and develop concentration skills by gently and firmly bringing the mind back to what is to be heard. Thus most of the time you have an opportunity to be aware of how one-pointed your mind is, and to practice developing concentration on whatever you are seeing, hearing, feeling, thinking, smelling, or tasting. When you are eating, how much are you attending to the sensations of eating? When you are reading, how often do you find that you have "completed" a paragraph or page and don't know what you read?

114

The same applies to mindfulness. At almost any instant you can practice being aware of body sensations, breathing, feelings, one-pointedness of mind, specific thoughts and images, intentions, and/or processes of the mind. You can be aware of the functioning and effects of the attachments. You can notice the opening and closing of your heart or mind. Thus situations like brushing your teeth, washing dishes, or driving a car are wonderful opportunities to develop mindfulness. Often people treat such routines as boring and distract themselves by day-dreaming, planning, listening to music, and other diversions. But these moments are rich with sensations to be mindful of. In addition, one can be mindful of the reactions to the sensations and the situation in general.

Thus throughout the day one can develop concentration and mindfulness. But you need to gradually build it up, doing it more and more, so you don't overwhelm yourself or make it an unpleasant task. Relax and have a good time. Some days you might wear a "reminder" such as a particular necklace or ring which reminds you to be more mindful whenever you notice it. As concentration and mindfulness are gradually cultivated throughout the day, and as mini-meditations are incorporated, the distinctions between when one is meditating and when one is not start to dissolve. What you do when meditating involves a widening range of situations and forms. Sometimes you are sitting on a cushion watching your breath. Sometimes you are raking leaves.

Throughout the day you can be aware of and cultivate opening the heart. For example, notice how open you are to experiencing reality as it is. How much do you distort reality to fit some model in your mind? How much do your judgments and attachments keep you from unconditionally accepting yourself or someone else? How can you better make friends with yourself? To what extent can you see the spiritual aspect of another person beyond his or her personality and behavior? "Namaste" is a common Hindu greeting in Nepal and India. It means, "I greet the spiritual within you."

In the Christian monastic tradition is the prayer of the heart or "Jesus prayer." This involves keeping Jesus ever present in the ground of one's being. This intense practice often involves invocations such as "Jesus" or "Lord Jesus Christ, Son of God, have mercy on me." By keeping Jesus ever in one's awareness, by always praying at one level of consciousness, one can control thoughts and temptations, guard and purify the mind, lose pre-occupations with the limited self, bring the holy spirit into the heart, and become one in spirit with Christ. Similar practices are the "practice of the presence of God" and the "remembrance of the name," both of which involve continual remembrance of God. Mahatma Gandhi practiced keeping the name "Ram" always on his mind. Ram is one of the Hindu manifestations of God.

Retrospection is a useful practice to help cultivate a more continual spiritual perspective. Retrospection is done near the end of each day. You quiet your mind and then try to maintain a meditative stance as you let the events of the day freely pass through your consciousness. This need only take about ten minutes; but it will vary from day to day and person to person. The purpose is to let issues resolve themselves, to see things more clearly when you are less pulled into them, and to notice the subtle attachments you overlooked earlier.

Finally, many people find that keeping a journal is a valuable aid in personal and transpersonal growth. The journal of writings and drawings can include many things, such as one or more of the following: a meditation log reporting daily perceptions, experiences, and thoughts about your meditation practice; an attachment log each day noting attachments of particular interest and significance and what you are learning about dealing with them; a dream diary kept by your bedside for recording dreams as soon afterward they occur as possible; and a daily or weekly spiritual journal in which you note ideas, lessons, quotes, reminders, etc. about your spiritual practice. Keeping a journal can help you think more clearly about your practices and notice patterns and interrelationships you might otherwise overlook. It can also help you see progress where you think there is none. Reading over a journal you have kept for a while gives you a good perspective of yourself.

The act of writing down things relating to problems may help you better define the issue, see resolutions, or come up with new ideas and perceptions about the problem. Sometimes the act of writing gives you a chance to release emotions. It can also be a way to put down and throw away some attachments, finished business, and old ideas.

So the serious practitioner of a spiritual/transpersonal path recognizes that the overall practice is applicable all the time. This is not instead of whatever else one does, but in addition to it and inclusive of it. Formal sitting meditation, mini-meditations, retrospection, and journal-keeping are some of the ways gradually to cultivate a more general and more continual spiritual perspective.

16

Retreats

It is very helpful for most people periodically to step out of their lives, to take a time-out from the game. This helps us get a better perspective on our life, to see and think more clearly about what we are doing. Meditation is a good and easy way to do this, but we occasionally need a bigger change of scene. We need periodically to get out of town, or some equivalent.

Vacations are a common way to do this and can be fun, interesting, stimulating, and a distraction from many of our usual concerns. When geographically far away, we can look back on our life differently and perhaps see things in a better perspective. But vacations often are so filled with activities that we do not have the opportunity really to step out of our life; rather, we just change the events in our life. People often return from vacations tired and stressed. Thus, although vacations can be therapeutic in many ways, they are seldom the optimal way to develop transpersonal perspective. Usually we are so caught up in the events of a vacation we have little time for spiritual practice.

So in terms of personal and transpersonal growth, it is helpful to take periodic retreats in which we step out of our routines and do not fill the time with events. Parents need time away

from the children, time they can devote to themselves and/or their spouses. And individuals need time alone, time to regroup, recenter, and intensify spiritual practices.

The retreat might be an afternoon each week in which we leave the daily routine and go for quiet drives and walks alone. The retreat might be a day each week in which we rest from the usual activities and cultivate the spiritual. This is one of the Judeo-Christian commandments.

Every now and then a retreat of a few days or more can be useful. This might involve staying in a motel in a nearby town, staying in the house of friends while they are away, camping out, or going to a lodge in a state park or church camp.

Retreat time is a time to be quiet and introspective, a time to get out of the melodrama of daily living and reflect on it. It is a time to quiet the mind and pull into the here and now. It is a time to let go of some past attachments and resolve to begin anew. Some of the time might be devoted to reading spiritual and/or inspirational materials, but the retreat should not be filled with reading. The retreat is an opportunity for intensive meditation practice.

Although much can be accomplished in daily meditation, even more can be accomplished by the addition of retreats in which one meditates for many hours a day for a number of days. In such intensive meditation one can reach depths that are hard to reach in shorter sessions. This will also facilitate daily practice, making it easier to achieve these levels again. In addition, powerful insights may arise during intense practice.

Of course, one has to build up to such intense practice. A beginner would probably have more negative than positive results from five days of intensive meditation. After you have been meditating regularly for a while, set aside a day in which you meditate for several hours. Alternate sitting and walking meditations in a pattern that works well for you. One pattern might be forty-five-minute sitting periods alternated with thirty-minute walking periods. Longer sitting periods can be good. Walking meditations can help overcome drowsiness that comes with sitting. Finding your own rhythm is important.

You can also set up your own intensive meditation retreat. Find a place such as those mentioned above, where you can be alone and undisturbed. Make living there as simple as possible. Eat the minimum amount necessary and stick to simple, basic foods. Avoid television, music, day-dreaming, and excessive or non-spiritual reading. Establish a simple routine of sleeping, eating, cleaning, and exercise. Perhaps you can provide a little spiritual input from books or tapes, but meditate as much as possible, alternating sitting and walking meditations.

Throughout the United States and the world there are many meditation retreat centers. Many are inexpensive and open to the public. Some are church sponsored; some are not. Some provide instruction in meditation; some just provide a place for you to meditate. If you are serious about meditation and wish to pursue the practice beyond the basics outlined in this book, it would be advantageous for you to seek personal instruction, such as is found at many meditation retreats.

When one has been out of the routine of life for a while, as when on vacation or retreat, one needs to attend carefully to re-entry. You don't want to jump back into your ordinary life as it was with the same old thoughts and feelings. Rather, you want to re-enter more gradually, being mindful of your old thoughts, reactions, habits, and attachments. Schedule your time so you can do this slowly. Don't arrive home late on Sunday and then start work early Monday. Try to keep your mind as quiet and aware for as long as possible. Avoid old attachments. Intentionally break undesired habits. Be a warrior. Approach the game of life with new clarity, compassion, and precision. Avoid getting pulled into the melodrama.

Slowly you will get pulled more and more into the dream of your daily life until eventually you will be asleep again. But the longer you stay awake during re-entry, the easier it will to be wake up again.

This book summarizes the practices for gradual awakening. These practices can improve daily living as well as leading to that which is beyond. There is little more you need to know. But you need to incorporate these practices, in whatever form is appropriate, into your daily living. You need to *do* the practices, not just think about them.

Of course, there is much more that could be said on any of the topics covered here and many more practices that could be useful to you. You should seek out those that you need and utilize those that your particular path leads you to. But the basics, as outlined in this book, are fairly universal; you will keep coming back to the basics. It is all very simple.

I wish you well on the journey and offer this book to help you along the way.

Appendix: Some
Basic Definitions

General Principles

(Chapters in parentheses discuss principles)

Make friends with yourself (2, 6, 9, 10, 15)
Accept unconditionally (2, 4, 6, 9, 10, 11, 13, 15)
Relax (9, 13, 15)
Be in the here and now (6, 7, 8, 9, 13, 15, 16)
Have a good time (4, 6, 8, 9, 12, 13, 15)

Common Traps

(Chapters in parentheses discuss principles)

Form vs. essence (1, 9, 13, 14, 15)
Reality vs. mind model (4, 5, 9, 10, 15)
Person vs. behavior (4, 9, 10, 15)
More is never enough (9, 10, 13)

Four Noble Truths (The Buddha)

1. Life is filled with dukkha (suffering/unsatisfactoriness).
2. The source of dukkha is craving (Chapter 10).
3. Dukkha ends when craving ceases.
4. The way to end dukkha and craving is the Eightfold Path.

Eight-Fold Path (The Buddha)

1. Right understanding (Buddhist and equivalent teachings)
2. Right thought (no lust, ill-will, or cruelty)

3. Right speech (constructive and helpful; no lying, gossip, or vanity)
4. Right action (moral, precise, aware)
5. Right livelihood (doesn't cause suffering)
6. Right effort (do it; the middle way)
7. Right mindfulness (Chapters 8 and 15)
8. Right concentration (Chapters 7 and 15)

"Right" = perfect, harmonious, in balance, conscious

Eight Limbs of Yoga (compiled by Patanjali)
1. Yama: abstention from evil conduct
2. Niyama: virtuous conduct
3. Asana: physical postures
4. Pranayama: control of breath and vital energy
5. Pratyahara: withdrawal of senses
6. Dharana: concentration
7. Dhyana: meditation
8. Samadhi: union with divine ground

Yama and Niyama (Yoga)

Non-violence
Non-stealing
Avoiding sexual excess, control over sexual cravings
Non-possessiveness, non-hoarding, non-greed
Truthfulness
Cleanliness and purity of body and mind
Practices to perfect body and mind
Contentment
Study of self and spiritual works
Surrender to God/ultimate truth

Five Basic Precepts (Buddhism)

Abstain from:
1. Killing
2. Stealing
3. Inappropriate sexual behavior
4. False and/or harmful speech
5. Intoxicating or mind-altering drugs, particularly ones causing heedlessness

Ten Commandments (Judaism/Christianity)

1. Have no other gods before the fundamental God
2. Do not construct or worship false gods or images of God
3. Do not take the name of God in vain
4. Do not work on the Sabbath (each seventh day) and keep it holy
5. Honor your father and mother
6. Do not kill
7. Do not commit adultery
8. Do not steal
9. Do not lie, particularly about others
10. Do not covet what is not yours

The Perennial Philosophy (ala Aldous Huxley)

1. The phenomenal world of matter and individualized consciousness, the world of things, animals, people, and gods, is a manifestation of a Divine Ground within which all partial realities have their being, and apart from which they would be nonexistent.
2. Humans are capable not merely of knowing about the Divine Ground by inference. They can also realize its existence by a direct intuition which is superior to discursive reasoning. This immediate knowledge unites the knower with what is known.
3. People possess a double nature, a phenomenal ego and an eternal Self, the latter being the spirit or spark of divinity within the soul. It is possible for a person to identify with the spirit and therefore the Divine Ground, which is of like nature with the spirit.
4. One's life on earth has only one end and purpose: to identify with the eternal Self and so come to unitive knowledge of the Divine Ground.

Suggested Reading

Many of the books in this list go in and out of print with various publishers. There are also many different translations of some of the non-English books, particularly classic spiritual texts. I cannot say which translation is the most "accurate" or "appropriate" for any particular reader.

The books are grouped by the following overlapping categories:

American Indians
Attachments/Addictions
Autobiographies
Buddhism and the Buddha
Buddhism: Tantric/Tibetan
Buddhism: Zen
Chakras and Kundalini
Christian Practice
Christian Theory
Consciousness
Death
Dreams
Happiness
Journals/Diaries
Judaism
Love
Meditation: Practice
Meditation: Theory and Research
Mindfulness/Vipassana
Mysticism/Enlightenment
References

Religion
Religious Classics
Self-improvement
Stories
Sufism
Taoism
Teachers: Contemporary
Transpersonal Psychology: General
Transpersonal Psychology: East and West
Yoga: General
Yoga: Hatha

American Indians

These books deal with the American Indian spiritual perspective, relationship to the Earth, and problems with the white man. Storm tells the philosophy of the Plains people through stories. Freesoul discusses Indian spiritual practices and symbols, including the ceremonial pipe and the medicine wheel.

Freesoul, J.R. *Breath of the invisible*. Quest Books, 1986.
McLuhan, T.C. *Touch the earth*. Outerbridge and Dienstfrey, 1971.
Niehardt, J.G. *Black Elk speaks*. Pocket Books, 1972.
Storm, H. *Seven arrows*. Ballantine, 1973.

Attachments/Addictions

Goleman surveys the "psychology of self-deception." Keyes has written many popular books about getting free from attachments. The Mauls' textbook summarizes many of the barriers to personal growth.

Goleman, D. *Vital lies, simple truths*. Simon & Schuster, 1985.
Keyes, K. *Handbook to higher consciousness*. Living Love Center, fifth edition, 1975.
————. & P. Keyes. *Gathering power through insight and love*. Living Love Publications, 1987.

Maul, G. & T. Maul. *Beyond limit: Ways to growth and freedom.* Scott, Foresman, 1983.

Autobiographies

The personal stories of people involved with pursuing a spiritual path and/or consciousness expansion within the contexts of Christianity (Merton, Roberts), American Indian (Castaneda), Buddhism (Hamilton-Merritt, Trungpa, Watts), yoga (Jones, Muktananda, Ram Dass, Swami Rama, Yogananda), psychedelic drugs (Castaneda, Lilly, Ram Dass, Watts), and "other" (Lilly, Merrell-Wolff, Watts).

Castaneda, C. *The teachings of Don Juan.* Ballantine Books, 1969. *A separate reality.* Simon & Schuster, 1971. *Journey to Ixtlan.* Simon & Schuster, 1972. *Tales of power.* Simon & Schuster, 1974.

Dass, Ram. *Be here now.* Lama Foundation, 1971.

Hamilton-Merritt, J. *A meditator's diary.* Pelican Books, 1979.

Jones, F. *The knee of listening.* Dawn Horse Press, 1972. *Garbage and the goddess.* Dawn Horse Press, 1974. (Jones later calls himself "Bubba Free John.")

Lilly, J. *The center of the cyclone.* Bantam Books, 1973.

Merrell-Wolff, F. *Pathways through to space.* Warner Books, 1976.

Merton, T. *The seven storey mountain.* Harcourt Brace Jovanovich, 1948.

Muktananda Paramahansa, Swami. *The play of consciousness.* S.Y.D.A. Foundation, 1974.

Rama, Swami. *Living with the Himalayan masters.* Himalayan International Institute of Yoga Science & Philosophy, 1978.

Roberts, B. *The experience of no-self.* Shambhala, 1984.

Trungpa, Chögyam. *Born in Tibet.* Random House, 1985.

Watts, A. *In my own way.* Vintage Books, 1972.

Yogananda, Paramahansa. *Autobiography of a Yogi.* Self-Realization Fellowship, 1946.

Buddhism and the Buddha

Rahula provides a good introduction to the Buddha and his teachings. Rice and Woodward provide some of the Buddha's teachings. Byles tells a story of the Buddha's life and teachings as it might be seen through a disciple's eyes. Conze and Ross overview some of the development and different schools of Buddhism, and the other three books are compilations of some of the vast Buddhist literature.

Burtt, E.A. *The teachings of the compassionate Buddha.* Mentor, 1955.

Byles, M.B. *Footprints of Gautama the Buddha.* Quest Books, 1967.

Conze, E. *Buddhism: Its essence and development.* Harper Colophon, 1975.

———, I.B. Horner, D. Snellgrove, & A. Waley. *Buddhist texts through the ages.* Harper Torchbooks, 1954.

Rahula, W. *What the Buddha taught.* Grove Press, enlarged edition, 1974.

Rice, S. *The Buddha speaks here and now.* Buddhist Publication Society, 1981. (Buddhist scriptures in contemporary idiom.)

Ross, N.W. *Buddhism: A way of life and thought.* Vintage Books, 1981.

Stryk, L. *World of the Buddha.* Grove Press, 1968.

Woodward, F.L. *Some sayings of the Buddha.* Oxford University Press, 1973.

Buddhism: Tantric/Tibetan

The book by Blofeld and the one by Guenther & Trungpa provide an introductory overview. Chögyam Trungpa, who died recently, and Tarthang Tulku, Tibetan Buddhists, have taught in the United States. The book by Guenther and the one by Hopkins are more academically philosophical and psychological.

Blofeld, J. *The tantric mysticism of Tibet.* E.P. Dutton, 1970.

Guenther, H.V. *Tibetan Buddhism in Western perspective.* Dharma Publishing, 1977.

———— & Chögyam Trungpa. *The dawn of tantra.* Shambhala, 1975.

Hopkins, J. *The tantric distinction.* Wisdom Publications, 1984.

Tarthang Tulku. *Gesture of balance.* Dharma Publishing, 1977.

Trungpa, Chögyam. *Journey without goal.* Prajna Press, 1981. *The myth of freedom.* Shambhala, 1976. *Cutting through spiritual materialism.* Shambhala, 1973.

Buddhism: Zen

During the 1950s and 1960s many books by Alan Watts and D. T. Suzuki were part of Zen's strong influx into the West. The books by Watts and Ross describe the Zen perspective and its influence. Kapleau and Sekida discuss Zen practice. And Suzuki's (not D. T. Suzuki) book is an excellent set of talks on Zen meditation and attitude. See also "Stories" category.

Kapleau, P. *The three pillars of Zen.* Anchor Books, expanded edition, 1980.

Ross, N.W. *The world of Zen: An East-West anthology.* Vintage Books, 1960.

Sekida, K. *Zen training.* Weatherhill, 1975.

Suzuki, S. *Zen mind, beginners mind.* Weatherhill, 1970.

Watts, A.W. *The way of Zen.* Vintage Books, 1957.

Chakras and Kundalini

Sannella describes some of the psychological problems associated with and/or confused with the rising of kundalini. The other books go further into the chakras and kundalini.

Motoyama, H. *Theories of the chakras: Bridge to higher consciousness.* Quest Books, 1981.

Pandit, M.P. *Kundalini yoga.* Ganesh & Co., 1968.

Sannella, L. *Kundalini—Psychosis or transcendence?* H. S. Dakin, 1976.

Scott, M. *Kundalini in the physical world.* Routledge & Kegan Paul, 1983.

Christian Practice

The books by French, Brother Lawrence, Bunyan, and à Kempis are classics in Christian living and practices, with the originals respectively over 100, 300, 300, and 400 years old. The books by French and Brother Lawrence are concerned with the practice of continual prayer, as mentioned in Chapter 15. Powell discusses the role of attitudes in Christian practice. The three-volume *Course in Miracles* was "dictated" to psychologist Helen Schucman by a "voice" claiming to be Jesus. These popular books encourage forgiveness and changes in attitudes and thoughts. See also the categories "Meditation: Practice" and "Journals/ Diaries."

A course in miracles. Foundation for Inner Peace, 1975.

Bunyan, J. *Pilgrim's progress.* Zondervan Publishing House, 1967.

French, R.M. (trans.). *The way of the pilgrim.* Ballantine Books, 1974.

Lawrence, Brother. *The practice of the presence of God.* Whitaker House, 1982.

Powell, J. *The Christian vision.* Argus Communications, 1984.

Thomas à Kempis. *The imitation of Christ.* Image Books, 1985 (Editor: H. C. Gardiner).

Christian Theory

To best understand the Bible it is useful to have a handbook, such as Eerdmans', to provide additional information, such as historical and cultural factors. Since what is included in the Bible was heavily influ-

enced by social and political forces, to better understand early Christianity and the potential breadth of
Christianity, it is helpful to consider early Christian
writings which were not included. The current best example is the gnostic gospels found at Nag Hammadi.
Pagels discusses these gospels, which are given in total
by Robinson.

Lewis is currently one of the most popular traditional
Christian writers. Jesuit paleontologist Teilhard de
Chardin provides a provocative theory of the biologi-
cal/spiritual evolution of man, which continues well
beyond where we are now. Fox argues for a creation-
centered Christian spirituality, as opposed to the dominant fall-redemption approach. Swami Prabhavananda
discusses the Sermon on the Mount from a Hindu/
yogic point of view.

Alexander, D. & P. Alexander (eds.). *Eerdmans' con-
cise Bible handbook*. Wm. B. Eerdmans, 1980.
Fox, M. *Original blessing*. Bear & Co., 1983.
Lewis, C.S. *Mere Christianity*. Macmillan, 1943.
Pagels, E. *The gnostic gospels*. Vintage Books, 1981.
Prabhavananda, Swami. *The Sermon on the Mount ac-
cording to Vedanta*. Mentor Book, 1972.
Robinson, J.M. (ed.). *The Nag Hammadi library*.
Harper & Row, 1981.
Teilhard de Chardin, P. The phenomenon of man.
Harper Torchbook, 1961.

Consciousness

Ornstein (1977), Pelletier, and Tart (1975) synthesize
some of our knowledge about consciousness. Lilly summarizes work with isolation tanks, while Masters and
Houston summarize what has been learned via psychedelic drugs. The other five books are collections of articles about consciousness.

Goleman, D. & R.J. Davidson (eds.). *Consciousness:
Brain, states of awareness, and mysticism*. Harper &
Row, 1979.

Lilly, J.C. *The deep self.* Warner Books, 1978.

Masters, R.E.L. & J. Houston. *The varieties of psychedelic experience.* Delta Book, 1966.

Ornstein, R.E. (ed.). *The nature of human consciousness.* W. H. Freeman, 1973.

————. *The psychology of consciousness.* Harcourt Brace Jovanovich, second edition, 1977.

Pelletier, K.R. *Toward a science of consciousness.* Delta Book, 1978.

Tart, C.T. (ed.). *Altered states of consciousness.* Wiley, 1969.

————. *States of consciousness.* E. P. Dutton, 1975.

White, J. (ed.). *The highest state of consciousness.* Anchor Books, 1972.

Wolman, B.B. & M. Ullmann (eds.). *Handbook of states of consciousness.* Van Nostrand Reinhold, 1986.

Death

Kübler-Ross discusses the psychological needs of the dying person. Levine considers how to die consciously, a spiritual approach to death. Moody surveys the experiences of people who almost died, some of whom were "clinically dead."

Kübler-Ross, E. *On death and dying.* Macmillan, 1970.

Levine, S. *Who dies?* Anchor Books, 1982.

Moody, R.A. *Life after life.* Bantam Book, 1976.

Dreams

Faraday discusses how to interpret dreams, Garfield how to plan and work with dreaming, and LaBerge how to "awake" while dreaming.

Faraday, A. *The dream game.* Perennial Library, 1976.

Garfield, P. *Creative dreaming.* Ballantine Books, 1976.

LaBerge, S. *Lucid dreaming.* Ballantine Books, 1986.

Happiness

These books offer various ideas about how to cultivate happiness, including unconditional acceptance

(Kaufman), reducing worry (Carnegie), Western perspectives (Houston), and Eastern perspectives (Watts).

Carnegie, D. *How to stop worrying and start living.* Pocket Book, 1953.

Houston, J.P. *The pursuit of happiness.* Scott Foresman, 1981.

Kaufman, B.N. *To love is to be happy with.* Fawcett Crest, 1977.

Watts, A.W. *The meaning of happiness.* Harper Colophon, 1979.

Journals/Diaries

Progoff describes how to use his "intensive journal" for personal and transpersonal growth. It is a structured journal with many components and exercises. Rainer shows how to use a journal for "self-guidance and expanded creativity." Kelsey covers "Christian growth through personal journal writing."

Kelsey, M. *Adventure inward.* Augsburg Publishing House, 1980.

Progoff, I. *At a journal workshop.* Dialogue House Library, 1975.

Rainer, T. *The new diary.* J. P. Tarcher, 1978.

Judaism

Williams provides a history of the Jewish people from 538 B.C. to 1500 A.D. Buber's book is a classic work in Hasidism, a movement of Jewish mysticism. Hoffman and Schachter pursue the intersection of Hasidism with contemporary psychology. The other books discuss the Kabbalah, a symbolic system of Jewish mysticism and occultism.

Buber, M. *I and thou.* Charles Scribner's Sons, 1970 (Walter Kaufman translator.).

Fortune, D. *The mystical Qabalah.* Ernest Benn, 1935.

Gonzalez-Wippler, M. *A Kabbalah for the modern world.* Bantam Book, 1977.

Hoffman, E. *The way of splendor.* Shambhala, 1981.

Ponce, C. *Kabbalah.* Quest Books, 1986.

Schachter, Z.M. & E. Hoffman, *Sparks of light.* Shambhala, 1983.

Waite, A.E. *The holy Kabbalah.* University Books, 1960.

Williams, J.G. *Judaism.* Quest Books, 1980.

Love

Various perspectives on the nature and cultivation of love.

Buscaglia, L. *Love.* Fawcett Crest, 1972.

Fromm, G. *The art of loving.* Harper & Row, 1956.

Hendricks, G. *Learning to love yourself.* Prentice-Hall, 1982.

Welwood, J. (ed.). *Challenge of the heart.* Shambhala, 1985.

Meditation: Practice

Le Shan's book is a good general introduction to meditation. Ellwood tells the beginner about quieting the mind via meditation. Solé-Leris provides an introduction to the concentration and mindfulness meditation practices of Theravadin Buddhism. Kelsey discusses Christian meditation, while Fleming elaborates on the classic Christian meditations of St. Ignatius. The book by de Mello is a unique blend of Buddhist mindfulness and Christian meditation (e.g., the St. Ignatius exercises). Other books on Buddhist meditation can be found under "Buddhism: Zen" and "Mindfulness/Vipassana."

de Mello, A. *Sadhana: A way to God.* Institute of Jesuit Sources, 1978.

Ellwood, R. *Finding the quiet mind.* Quest Books, 1983.

Fleming, D.L. *The spiritual exercises of St. Ignatius.* Institute of Jesuit Sources, 1978.

Kelsey, M. *The other side of silence.* Paulist Press, 1976.

Le Shan, L. *How to meditate.* Bantam Book, 1975.

Solé-Leris, A. *Tranquility and insight.* Shambhala, 1986.

Meditation: Theory and Research

Goleman surveys the many different approaches to meditation within the major world systems. White's book is a collection of articles on different aspects of meditation. Carrington and Shapiro & Walsh deal with contemporary Western research approaches to meditation.

Carrington, P. *Freedom in meditation.* Anchor Press, 1978.

Goleman, D. *The varieties of the meditative experience.* E. P. Dutton, 1977.

Shapiro, D.H. & R.N. Walsh (eds.). *Meditation: Classic and contemporary perspectives.* Aldine, 1984.

White, J. (ed.). *What is meditation?* Anchor Books, 1974.

Mindfulness/Vipassana

Books dealing with mindfulness and vipassana based on classic Theravadin Buddhist teachings and practices. Dhiravamsa, Nyanaponika Thera, and Soma Thera overview such approaches. The *Visuddhi Magga* is an outstanding encyclopedia of Buddhist doctrine and meditation practices compiled by Buddhaghosa about the fifth century A.D. Goldstein's book is a set of talks and instructions from a meditation retreat. The other books are from respected contemporary Eastern teachers (Mahasi Sayadaw, S. N. Goenka, Achaan Chah).

Buddhaghosa. *Visuddi Magga (The path of purification).* Buddhist Publication Society, 1975. Translator Bhikkhu Nanamoli.

Dhiravamsa. *The way of non-attachment.* Schocken Books, 1977.

Goldstein, J. *The experience of insight.* Shambhala, 1983.

Hart, W. *The art of living: Vipassana meditation as taught by S. N. Goenka.* Harper & Row, 1987.

Kornfield, J. & P. Breiter. *A still forest pool: The insight meditation of Achaan Chah.* Quest Books, 1985.

Sayadaw, Mahasi. *Practical insight meditation.* Followed by *The progress of insight.* Buddhist Publication Society, 1980 & 1978.

Thera, Nyanaponika. *The heart of Buddhist meditation.* Rider & Co., 1962.

Thera, Soma. *The way of mindfulness.* Buddhist Publication Society, fourth edition, 1975.

Mysticism/Enlightenment

White's book is a good collection of articles about enlightenment. Stace provides a collection of writings from the great mystics of various traditions. Roberts is a contemporary American Christian mystic. Merrell-Wolff describes a philosophical model of the highest level of consciousness. Bucke's and Underhill's books are early classics in the field. Related material can be found under the category "consciousness."

Bucke, M. *Cosmic consciousness.* E. P. Dutton, 1969.

Merrell-Wolff, F. *The philosophy of consciousness without an object.* Julian Press, 1973.

Roberts, B. *The path to no-self.* Shambhala, 1985.

Stace, W.T. *The teachings of the mystics.* Mentor Books, 1960.

Underhill, E. *Mysticism.* E. P. Dutton, 1961.

White, J. (ed.). *What is enlightenment?* J. P. Tarcher, 1985.

References

The dictionaries by Jack and Reese help define spiritual terms. Popenoe's book is a massive annotated bib-

liography of the types of books in this suggested
reading section. *The New Consciousness Sourcebook,*
previously *The Spiritual Community Guide,* is a book
that comes out every few years listing spiritual groups,
training centers, classified ads, etc. Henderson surveys
many of the personal and transpersonal growth groups
of the 1970s. The last half of Ram Dass's book is a
directory of American retreat centers and places of
meditation instruction.

Dass, Ram. *Journey of awakening: A meditator's guide-
book.* Bantam Book, 1978.
Henderson, C.W. *Awakening.* Prentice-Hall, 1975.
Jack, A. *The new age dictionary.* Kanthaka Press, 1976.
Khalsa, P.S. (ed.). *The new consciousness sourcebook.*
Spiritual Community Publications.
Popenoe, C. *Inner development.* Yes! Inc., 1979.
Reese, W.L. *Dictionary of philosophy and religion.*
Humanities Press, 1980.

Religion

Schuon and Smith discuss the fundamental spiritual
commonalities of religions, including the perennial
philosophy. Wilber relates religion to his general devel-
opmental/consciousness model (see "Teachers: Contemporary"). Lilly surveys the many beliefs that people
take for God. James's book is an early classic in the
psychology of religion. Stapleton's science fiction story
tells of an evolving God who creates a succession of
universes. Spilka, Hood, and Gorsuch provide a current
textbook on the psychology of religion.

James, W. *The varieties of religious experience.* Mentor
Books, 1958.
Lilly, J.C. *Simulations of God.* Bantam Books, 1976.
Schuon, F. *The transcendent unity of religions.* Quest
Books, 1984.
Smith, H. *Forgotten truth: The primordial tradition.*
Harper Colophon, 1977.
Spilka, B., R.W. Hood, & R.L. Gorsuch. *The psychol-
ogy of religion.* Prentice-Hall, 1985.

Stapleton, O. *Star maker*. Penguin Books, 1972.
Wilber, K. *A sociable God*. Shambhala, 1983.

Religious Classics

Bhagavad-Gita. One of the world's most loved spiritual works. Instruction in yoga within the context of a great epic story. J. Mascaro, Penguin Books, 1962. Swami Prabhavananda, Mentor Books, 1944. Shri Purohit Swami, Vintage Books, 1977.

The Dhammapada. Some sayings of the Buddha. P. Lal, Farrar, Straus & Giroux, 1967. T. Byrom, Vintage Books, 1976.

Holy Bible. The basic text of the Judeo-Christian religions. A collection of folklore, history, letters, laws, ceremonies, hymns, prayers, sermons, odes, proverbs, and essays. The King James version is still preferred by many, though the Revised Standard Version is widely used in theological studies. The gospel of John is perhaps the gospel closest to the perennial philosophy; it is the most "mystical" of the gospels.

The Koran (Quran). The holy scripture of Islam, the record of Mohammed's oral teachings. J. M. Rodwell, translator, Everyman's Library, 1974.

Tao Teh Ching (The way of life). The basic scripture of Taoism attributed to Lao Tzu. R. B. Blakney, Mentor Books, 1955. W. Bynner, Capricorn Books, 1944. G. Feng & J. English, Vintage Books, 1972.

Self-Improvement

Books for "cleaning house" (Chapter 11), dealing with common practical psychological problems.

Martin, R.A. & Poland, E.Y. *Learning to change*. McGraw-Hill, 1980.
Mikulas, W.L. *Skills of living*. University Press of America, 1983.
Shapiro, D.H. *Precision Nirvana*. Prentice-Hall, 1978.

Watson, D.L. & R.G. Tharp. *Self-directed behavior.* Brooks/Cole, fourth edition, 1985.

Williams, R.L. & J.D. Long. *Toward a self-managed life style.* Houghton Mifflin, third edition, 1983.

Yates, B.T. *Self-management.* Wadsworth, 1985.

Stories

These books are all collections of short stories intended to stimulate spiritual understanding. Jataka stories are legends of former lives of the Buddha, often as an animal. Shah's book is a collection of Sufi stories.

de Mello, A. *The song of the bird.* Image Books, 1984.

Kahn, N.I. Twenty Jataka tales. Inner Traditions International, 1985.

Reps, P. *Zen flesh, Zen bones.* Anchor Books, 1957.

Salajan, I. *Zen comics.* Charles E. Tuttle, I in 1974, II in 1982.

Shah, I. *The pleasantries of the incredible Mulla Nasrudin.* E. P. Dutton, 1971. (The first of four such collections.).

Van Over, R. *Taoist tales.* Mentor, 1973.

Sufism

Books about Sufism, the mystical side of Islam.

Lings, M. *What is sufism?* University of California Press, 1977.

Schuon, F. *Sufism: Veil and quintessence.* World Wisdom Books, 1981.

Shah, I. *The Sufis.* Anchor Books, 1971.

Taoism

The basic work here is the *Tao Teh Ching* (see "Religious Classics") followed by Chuang Tsu's *Inner Chapters.* Wei's translation and commentary on the *Tao Teh Ching* is in terms of meditation and mysticism.

Blofeld, J. *Gateway to wisdom*. Shambhala, 1980. (Taoist and Mahayana Buddhist practices).

————. *Taoism: The road to immortality*. Shambhala, 1978.

Feng, G. & J. English (translators). *Chuang Tsu Inner Chapters*. Vintage Books, 1974.

Watts, A. *Tao: The watercourse way*. Pantheon Books, 1975.

Wei, H. *The guiding light of Lao Tzu*. Quest Books, 1982.

Teachers: Contemporary

Below is a sample of books from teachers who have been influential in American spirituality in the last twenty-five years. Da Free John (a.k.a. Franklin Jones, Bubba Free John, Da Love-Ananda) is an American teacher who offers himself as a fully realized master. Krishnamurti was a highly respected teacher who encouraged mindfulness and getting free from the search. Merton was a Christian contemplative who incorporated many Eastern perspectives. Ram Dass (Richard Alpert) is a popular and eclectic American bhakti yogi. Watts was a very popular and readable explainer of Eastern perspectives. All have autobiographies listed in that category, except Krishnamurti for whom Mary Lutyens and Pupul Jayakar have written biographies.

Contemporary Buddhist teachers can be found under the Tantric/Tibetan, Zen, and Mindfulness/Vipassana categories. Contemporary yoga teachers include Sri Nisargadatta Maharaj, Swami Muktananda, Swami Narayanda, Swami Rama, and Swami Satchidananda.

Da Free John. *The Dawn Horse testament of Heart-Master Da Free John*. Dawn Horse Press, 1985.

Dass, Ram. *The only dance there is*. Anchor Books, 1974.

————. *Grist for the mill*. Bantam Books, 1979.

Krishnamurti, J. *The first and last freedom*. Harper & Row, 1954.

————. *Think on these things.* Harper & Row, 1964.

————. *The second Penguin Krishnamurti reader.* Penguin Books, 1970 (M. Lutyens, editor).

————. *The awakening of intelligence.* Harper & Row, 1973.

————. *The flame of attention.* Harper & Row, 1984.

Merton, T. *No man is an island.* Harcourt, Brace Jovanovich, 1955.

————. *Mystics and Zen masters.* Delta Book, 1961.

————. *A Thomas Merton reader.* Image Book, 1974. (T. P. McDonnell, editor).

Watts, A.W. *The book.* Collier Books, 1966.

————. *Cloud-hidden, whereabouts unknown.* Vintage Books, 1974.

————. *The essence of Alan Watts.* Celestial Arts, 1977.

Transpersonal Psychology: General

Maslow and Van Dusen wrote two of the earlier books in Western transpersonal psychology. Assagioli's psychosynthesis was one of the first Western psychotherapies to give significant weight to the transpersonal. Ferrucci gives many exercises within the psychosynthesis tradition. Metzner surveys many of the models/analogies of human growth and transformation. Wilber is one of the foremost contemporary theorists in transpersonal psychology. Ram Dass and Gorman present stories and discussion of people in the helping professions and related personal and spiritual issues. The other books are collections of articles about transpersonal theory and research.

Assagioli, R. *Psychosynthesis.* Penguin Books, 1976.

Boorstein, S. (ed.). *Transpersonal psychotherapy.* Science and Behavior Books, 1980.

Dass, Ram & P. Gorman. *How can I help?* Knopf, 1985.

Dean, S.R. (ed.). *Psychiatry & mysticism.* Nelson-Hall, 1975.

Ferrucci, P. *What we may be.* J. P. Tarcher, 1982.

Maslow, A. *The farther reaches of human nature.* Penguin Books, 1976.

Metzner, R. *Opening to inner light.* J. P.Tarcher, 1986.

Tart, C. T. (ed.). *Transpersonal psychologies.* Harper & Row, 1975.

Van Dusen, W. *The natural depth in man.* Harper & Row, 1972.

Walsh, R.N. & F. Vaughan (eds.). *Beyond ego.* J. P. Tarcher, 1980.

Welwood, J. (ed.). *The meeting of the ways.* Schocken Books, 1979.

Wilber, K. *The Atman project.* Quest Books, 1980.

————. *Up from Eden.* Shambhala, 1983.

————. *Eye to eye.* Anchor Books, 1983 (This book is the best overview by Wilber).

Transpersonal Psychology: East and West

These books deal with the interfacing of Western and Eastern psychological/spiritual perspectives. Watts is fairly general, Swami Rama and Swami Ajaya emphasize yoga, and the other three emphasize Buddhism.

Ajaya, Swami. *Psychotherapy East and West.* Himalayan Publishers, 1983.

Fromm, E., D.T. Suzuki & R. DeMartino. *Zen Buddhism and psychoanalysis.* Harper & Row, 1960.

Katz, N. (ed.). *Buddhist and Western psychology.* Prajna Press, 1983.

Rama, Swami, R. Ballentine, & Swami Ajaya. *Yoga and psychotherapy.* Himalayan Institute, 1976.

Spiegelman, J.M. & M. Miyuki. *Buddhism and Jungian psychology.* Falcon Press, 1985.

Watts, A.W. *Psychotherapy East and West.* Ballantine Books, 1969.

Yoga: General

The books by Eliade, by Prabhavananda and Isherwood (1969), and by Taimni deal with yoga in general and the work of Patanjali. The books by Swami Rama and Wood describe some of the different paths of yoga (see Chapter 13). The other three books introduce three classic yogis, Aurobindo, Ramana Maharshi, and Shankara. See also the category "Chakras and Kundalini."

Eliade, M. *Patanjali and yoga*. Schocken Books, 1975.

————. *Yoga: Immortality and freedom*. Princeton University Press, second edition, 1970.

Maharshi, Ramana. *The spiritual teaching of Ramana Maharshi*. Shambhala, 1972.

McDermott, R. *The essential Aurobindo*. Schocken Books, 1973.

Prabhavananda, Swami & C. Isherwood. *How to know God: The yoga aphorisms of Patanjali*. Mentor, 1969.

————. *Shankara's crest-jewel of discrimination*. Mentor Books, 1970.

Rama, Swami. *Choosing a path*. Himalayan Publishers, 1982.

Taimni, I.K. *The science of yoga*. Quest Books, 1967.

Wood, E. *Seven schools of yoga*. Quest Books, 1973.

Yoga: Hatha

Books on hatha yoga including the postures *(asanas)* and working with the breath and vital energy *(pranayama)*.

Hittleman, R. *Introduction to yoga*. Bantam Books, 1969.

Iyengar, B.K.S. *Light on yoga*. Schocken Books, revised edition, 1977.

————. *The concise light on yoga*. Schocken Books, 1982.

Narayanananda, Swami. *The secrets of prana, pranayama, and yoga-asanas*. N.U. Yoga Trust, 5th edition, 1979.

Samskrti & Veda. *Hatha yoga*. Himalayan Institute, second edition, 1987 (first of two manuals).

Rama, Swami. *Path of fire and light: Advanced practices of yoga*. Himalayan Publishers, 1986.

————, R. Ballentine, & A. Hymes. *Science of breath.*
Himalayan Institute, 1979.
Vishnudevananda, Swami. *The complete illustrated
book of yoga.* Pocket Book, 1972.

About the Author

William M. Mikulas is Professor of Psychology at the University of West Florida at Pensacola, where he teaches courses in transpersonal psychology and Buddhist psychology as well as more traditional courses. He has published six books, the most recent of which is *Skills in Living*, a precursor to this book. He has published numerous articles, including ones on such subjects as "Buddhism and Behavior Modification" and "Four Noble Truths of Buddhism as Related to Behavior Therapy."

Dr. Mikulas received his Ph.D. in General Psychology and Behavior Modification at the University of Michigan, where he also earned his M.A. and B.A. degrees. He has served as Visiting Professor at the University of Nevada and in Thailand. He was chosen for the distinguished research award and also for the distinguished teaching award at West Florida.

QUEST BOOKS
are published by
The Theosophical Society in America,
Wheaton, Illinois 60189-0270,
a branch of a world organization
dedicated to the promotion of brotherhood and
the encouragement of the study of religion,
philosophy, and science, to the end that man may
better understand himself and his place in
the universe. The Society stands for complete
freedom of individual search and belief.
In the Classics Series well-known
theosophical works are made
available in popular editions.

Quest publishes books on Healing, Health and Diet, Occultism and Mysticism, Philosophy, Transpersonal Psychology, Reincarnation, Religion, The Theosophical Philosophy, Yoga and Meditation. Two popular titles from the above categories include:

The Silent Encounter *Edited by Virginia Hanson*
A book about your mystical nature and how and why you could suddenly become aware of life's unity.

Whispers From the Other Shore *By Ravi Ravindra*
How religions help and hinder us in the search for our center of being.

Available from:
The Theosophical Publishing House
306 West Geneva Road, Wheaton, Illinois 60187